UNSHAKEABLE JOY

A TRUE STORY OF STEADFAST FAITH IN LOSS

CAMERON DODD

To my pastors at Grace Bible Church in Tempe, Arizona, whom God used to equip both my husband and me for such a difficult time. We were well-prepared.

CAMERON DODD

CONTENTS

Introduction

A few years into my marriage, I remember reading a horrifying article about a Christian woman whose child had died in a tragic hit-and-run accident in their neighborhood.

I can't quite recall if it was an interview with her or a blog she had written, but I remember vividly her response to these unimaginable circumstances. She still held to her profession of faith, but there was so much bitterness, so much anger, and not much peace or hope for the future.

There was certainly no joy.

That might sound like a strange thing to look for in such distressing circumstances—joy—but having read my Bible a few times, I knew that God makes promises to believers when it comes to having joy in trials.

After reading that article, I walked away disturbed.

James 1:2-3 tells us: "Count it all *joy*, my brothers, when you meet trials of various kinds, for you know the testing of your faith produces steadfastness."

Similarly, Paul, who endured much suffering himself, declares in Romans 5:3-4 that not only do we have peace with God through Jesus Christ, but: "Not only that, but we *rejoice* in our sufferings, knowing that suffering produces endurance, and endurance produces character, and character produces hope."

It seemed to me that if the gospel was enough to solve our biggest problem—our sin and eternal separation from God—it should certainly be sufficient for the comparatively smaller problems of this earthly life.

Theologically, I was sure the gospel should be enough.

But experientially, I had nothing to point to. I had never been through something so severe, so painful. What did I know?

I know now.

Let me be clear what this book is not.

This book is *not* a how-to book about how to have joy in trials. Although, I suppose if one were to read closely enough, they might learn by one man's example how to do just that.

This book is *not* a manual for how to become a missionary or persevere on the mission field. Nor is it a book about how to deal with grief, cancer, or death.

Although, again, all of those things live within these pages.

What this book is, is the story of how one man was handed devastating circumstances, and the gospel was *enough*.

Enough for him to endure suffering not only with courage and conviction, but with *joy*.

We read about Christian heroes of the faith like the Apostle Paul, Jim Elliot, William Tyndale and the like and we wonder at their faith and their fortitude. We marvel at their willingness not just to live for the gospel, but to die for it as well! And we wonder...

...*Could I do that?* **Would** *I do that?*

If disaster were to befall me tomorrow, if that phone call were to come, that knock at the door, would I hold on to my faith? Would it hold onto me?

I am convinced that one of the kindest things God can give a believer is a trial. Because here's the thing: if your faith is never tested, how do you know if it's real?

That verse in James tells us that trials are not only designed to test our faith and prove it to be real, but that they're also designed to *strengthen* it. Like a tree that produces stress wood only in strong winds, trials produce endurance in the believer's faith.

What a boon to our soul to emerge from a trial and see our faith still standing fast! Like having a Category-5 hurricane tear through your town only to have your house still stand after it leaves, the foundation of your faith is proved to be stronger than the worst of storms.

Matt Dodd was a man whose life had been changed by the gospel of Jesus Christ. Anyone who knew him would have told you two things about him: he was ridiculously joyful, and he loved Jesus. He was a man whose faith did not just survive devastating circumstances but was made more steadfast because of them.

But perhaps the most encouraging thing about Matt was that he did not start out as a super mature, steadfast follower of Christ.

His faith began as the rest of us: small but sure.

Lots of enthusiasm for the gospel, but not as much theology or stability. Jesus said in Matthew 17:20, "If you have faith like a grain of mustard seed, you will say to this mountain, 'Move from here to there,' and it will move, and nothing will be impossible for you."

The point there being not that our faith gives us supernatural powers, but that our faith—even the tiniest bit—gives us access to the Source of *all* power. Nothing is impossible for the one who has faith because nothing is impossible with God.

Matt began his life with Christ with just a small bit of real, genuine faith. And God was faithful to grow that faith bit by bit, year after year, as Matt read his Bible and walked in obedience to Him.

It was not an accident or a miracle that Matt was able to go through a difficult trial and remain steadfast. It was the result of many years of reading God's Word and not just knowing its promises (like James 1!) but believing them. He was able to suffer and remain steadfast —not just in his theology but in his joy—not because he was so great, but because the God in whom he believed was.

As someone who has been on the receiving end of *that* phone call and everything that followed, I can tell you I was so encouraged to see that no matter how deep the darkness of his circumstances, Matt's confidence in God's character and His promises remained unchanged, undiminished, and undimmed.

I have written this book that others might be equally encouraged, not by the faithfulness of Matt Dodd, but by the faithfulness of the God who upheld Matt Dodd.

We live in a world with scary things. How are we not to fear them?

Matt's answer was because we know the One in control of all those things and believe that He has promised good to all who trust in Him (Rom. 8:28). He believed that his biggest problem had already been solved by Jesus on the cross and that everything else paled in comparison.

Is the gospel enough to sustain a believer when bad news comes?

Is it possible for one's faith to remain unshaken when everything falls down around them?

My hope is that in reading this book you might find the answer to be a resounding yes!

But only if your hope, your joy, is staked to something immoveable. *Someone* immoveable.

One day while sitting in the hospital, about five months before he died, I was reading Matt one of the Facebook posts I had written to update our friends and family.

"That's good," he said, nodding. "Keep writing, Cameron. We'll write when we're encouraged, and we'll read when we're discouraged."

This book is my attempt to do just that.

To give you a glimpse at a man who in himself had nothing, but who in Jesus had everything.

To all who are uncertain about the future, to all who wonder if their faith will hold in tragedy, may you read this and be encouraged that when all else fails, God never does. When our strength is gone and our footing gives way, He is faithful to hold fast the faith He so preciously purchased in the first place.

Perhaps you're reading this book and would say you are not a Christian. My hope is that by reading about the kind of joy this man had in living and dying, the question might be sparked, "But *how?*" And perhaps be led to make the God of Matt Dodd your own.

Shortly after his diagnosis, Matt prayed this:

"God, whatever your will is, please use these circumstances to fight our sin, become more holy, love You more, hope in heaven, and trust You. Please God, may we not be shaken by this!"

God was faithful to answer this prayer. Matt wasn't shaken by his circumstances because the foundation of his faith was unshakeable.

May all who read this book marvel at the strength of that foundation and desire to make it their own.

Prologue

The MRI was on a Monday.

My husband, Matt Dodd, and I, along with our four kids, were four months into a furlough from the mission field in our home state of Arizona.

In the midst of embracing relatives and making plans to return to our village back in Papua New Guinea, something odd began happening to Matt.

It started with his left hand going numb every once in a while.

Then the left side of his face.

The feeling would always return after a few minutes, but its unsettling effect would continue.

And there was more.

Sometimes, his left hand would feel like it needed to be doing something, but Matt didn't know what, so he would just walk around the house, squeezing his hands together until the feeling went away.

And then Disneyland happened.

While on this family vacation, Matt had the terrifying experience of seeing what was actually happening in one half of his vision, and uncontrollable flashes of dreams he had once had in the other.

This lasted for six hours.

By the end of the day, Matt was more than anxious.

He was scared.

We met with a neurologist soon after, but the doctor wasn't concerned. All of these symptoms, he assured us, were likely the result of Matt's migraines, something he had dealt with since college.

But we scheduled an MRI just to be safe.

Taking our cue from the neurologist, Matt and I were not worried. On the day of the MRI, I was at a playdate with our kids on the other side of town when I got the call.

"It was bad news," Matt said, raw unease lacing his words.

He told me how everything about the MRI was routine until the technicians had suddenly pulled him out of the scan partway through, palpable concern etched on their faces.

They injected him with contrast, muttering vague explanations as to why, before putting him back into the machine.

The second time around, the MRI ran for the full length of time.

When Matt was taken out of the machine, instead of being sent home to wait for results, he was asked to sit in a chair right outside the room for the on-site doctor.

Minutes later, the doctor appeared and gave Matt the news that would change his life forever.

The scan had revealed that there were over a dozen tumors in his brain.

Most likely, it was metastasized cancer originating somewhere else in his body.

The situation was emergent, as the scan had also revealed that one of the tumors had already bled once on his brain. The doctor told Matt he needed to go to the emergency room at Barrow Neurological Center in Phoenix immediately. Was there someone nearby that could drive him?

Matt's first phone call was to my mom, who lived less than a mile from the outpatient testing center where he was and with whom he shared a close relationship, to ask if she could drive him since I was on the other side of town.

His second phone call was to me.

I drove to meet him at the emergency room with shaking hands and a pounding heart. I felt as though the floor had just dropped out from underneath both of us.

Outside of the obvious threat to Matt's life, other serious implications hit me as I threaded my way across freeways to central Phoenix.

For one, we had nowhere to live.

Our home was no longer in the United States, but in a remote mountain village in Papua New Guinea. Everything we owned was there.

Expecting to only be here for a few months, we had brought only clothes with us and were staying with a family from our church.

Where would we live?

And there were other implications.

We were missionaries, just two years into our work in Papua New Guinea. I thought of the house we had built there, the people we had loved there, the language we had begun to learn there—and knew in an instant that we would not be returning.

Everything that we had planned for and prayed for and sold all we had for suddenly became a baton that would need to be passed along to someone else.

Assuming there *was* someone else.

Would the work we had started there even continue?

What about our four sweet kids?

Alone in the minivan, music off, heart pounding, I sought the Lord.

He answered not with a voice from heaven, but by calling to mind a multitude of verses. Verses like Psalm 115:3, "Our God is in the heavens; he does all that he pleases" and Psalm 119:68, "You are good and do good."

God's character had not changed. His plan had not changed. He was still sovereign, and He was still good. These truths were a cloak of assurance around me as I drove. I was not alone.

When I arrived at the hospital, I found my husband sitting on a gurney in the hallway of the emergency room, saying the exact same thing. There he sat, as nurse after nurse tried in vain to get an IV into his arm, smiling and declaring to each visitor that came through, "You guys, nothing has really changed. Whatever this is, we're still saved, and God is still good!"

As the scans and tests began, answers eventually came.

Stage IV lung cancer.

A terminal diagnosis.

For years, Matt had been praying that he would not waste his life. His desire had always been that when death did come for him, that it might be somehow for Christ—be it through persecution, martyrdom, or some other means.

Within minutes of hearing this diagnosis, Matt resolved that if this were the means by which God had appointed for him to die, he wanted it to be for Christ. His prayer was that, in cancer, he might be a living embodiment of Paul's words in Philippians 1:20. That he would "not be at all ashamed, but that with full courage now as always Christ will be honored in my body, whether by life or death."

Over the next six months, he did just that.

Though his circumstances went from bad to worse, he had courage to face them, seeing and declaring God's faithfulness every step of the way…until he took his last.

Matt didn't die a martyr, but he did die with his whole life pointing to Christ. The Shepherd who had called him was faithful to keep him until he was called home.

Part I

From the Desert to the Jungle

CHAPTER 1

God, Is This the Girl I'm Supposed to Marry?

The night I met Matt Dodd, I was clinging to the last fraying strands of my metaphorical rope.

And my grip was slipping.

Twenty years old and about to enter my third year of college, I was a self-proclaimed Christian but had been living a lifestyle that was anything but. I knew that I was lost, empty, miserable—knew that if Christianity was so great, I was missing something—while at the same time trying my best to feel none of those things.

With my ever-present smile plastered on my face, I sauntered into my friend, Jeff's, house on a hot July night in 2004 in Phoenix for a friendly poker tournament, fully expecting to leave in ten minutes.

I took my seat at the long, round dining table full of strangers and glanced around.

My friend since high school, Jeff, was famous for bringing eclectic groups of people together from different parts of his life, and tonight's group was no exception. There were old friends from high school like me, people he had met while studying abroad in Cambridge, and new acquaintances from Phoenix.

I looked to my left and froze.

Brown hair, brown eyes—it was the guy that I had been on a not-so-successful date with the other night.

Awkward.

I quickly swung my eyes to see who was on my right, instantly relieved to see it was a guy I didn't know.

Always interested in dating someone new, I took a longer look at the wild, curly hair and the too-tight T-shirt next to me, and decided I wasn't interested.

With one eye on the clock, I played the first hand.

"So, how do you know Jeff?" I heard the too-tight T-shirt ask me.

I answered, not terribly interested in the conversation, until something curious began to happen.

Up until this point in my life, I was pretty much the funniest person that I knew.

But somehow, for every witty comment or clever retort I had, this guy had two. Worse, I was having trouble keeping up—an experience I hadn't had before.

Within minutes, I was laughing harder than I had in a long time.

Suddenly, the game at the table I most wanted to win had nothing to do with cards.

Who *was* this guy?

I would learn that his name was Matt Dodd.

Twenty-three years old, newly graduated from Arizona State University with a bachelor's in Computer Science and going back for his master's, he had bright blue eyes, gauged ears, and a great smile.

And he was terrible at poker.

As the minutes ticked by, long beyond my expected departure time, the conversation turned to religion, and I learned that Matt was a Christian.

Since I was perpetually looking for a new church to attend, I asked where he went.

"East Valley Bible Church Tempe, by ASU," Matt answered, unbothered as he lost yet another hand.

"Could I come with you this Sunday?" I asked casually, studying the cards in my hand.

"You could, but I don't know if that would make sense," he said, his brow furrowing. "There's a campus way closer to where you live."

Inwardly, I rolled my eyes.

Maybe he wasn't as quick as I thought he was.

"Sure, but I wouldn't *know* anyone at that campus," I emphasized.

After several *long* minutes of me explaining why the Tempe campus was preferable, he shrugged, said of course, and we exchanged phone numbers.

I rattled mine off first, and he started to laugh.

"What?" I said.

"Are you serious?" he asked.

"Yeah," I returned. "Why?"

"Because that's my number," he replied, smiling and shaking his head. "Except for one digit."

Matt would tell me later that in that moment he thought, "God, is this the girl I'm supposed to marry?"

Spoiler alert: the answer was yes.

MOWING THE LAWN WITHOUT A SHIRT ON

Two days later, Matt called and invited me to play soccer with him and some friends.

He was living in a house a stone's throw away from Arizona State University with a bunch of other guys.

And by 'a bunch', I mean, more than should have been living in that house. It was Matt, his friend Nate, Creech, Costa and T.J., who slept in the closet…but I digress.

I pulled up to Matt's house and saw him mowing the lawn without his shirt on.

This was the tipping point for me because Matt was in very good shape.

I would later learn that his choice of activity during my arrival was no accident, but regardless, I was sold.

The soccer game ended up being cancelled, so Matt suggested we go for a run up Arizona State University's "A" mountain instead.

Even if the weather had been beautiful, this would never have been my suggestion. Seeing as it was a sweltering night on the 29th of July in Phoenix, the internal resistance was that much greater. But I wanted to be a good sport, so off we went.

I was determined to keep up with him all the way up the mountain, but this idea was quickly abandoned as I realized the trail was about a mile straight up the mountain on a paved path with a whole bunch of stairs.

And since Matt's pace seemed to be full-on *sprinting*, I swallowed my pride and eventually waved him ahead of me.

Several long minutes and many side cramps later, I made it to the top where the twinkling lights of Tempe, Arizona greeted me.

We bantered as we began our walk back through ASU's campus, and the more we talked, the more we realized we had in common. In addition to our phone numbers being nearly identical, we discovered that we had each had very specific, similar, crazy adventures.

We had both taken a whitewater rafting trip through a company called Noah's Ark in Colorado, for example. We had both chased a golf cart up the hills of Catalina Island.

We also shared the same crazy enthusiasm for life, like spontaneously swimming in a campus fountain for a minute before continuing our walk.

But as we ambled past the darkened buildings, our conversation turned more serious.

"So," I began, asking one of my go-to questions, "Tell me your life story."

I had asked many people that question, but the answer that this curly-headed, goofy, wild-as-me boy gave changed my life forever. Because the answer he gave wasn't just his life story; it was his testimony.

READING HIS BIBLE *JUST BECAUSE HE WANTED TO*

Matt had grown up in the small northern Arizona town of Prescott with his mom, Teresa, and older sister, Jill, who was pretty much his best friend.

His parents had divorced when he was two and had both re-married, giving him two half-brothers, Blake and George. He loved his family, he said, and was always eager to get together with them.

He had moved down to Phoenix with his mom when he was thirteen but had a rough time in his public junior high with fights and rough kids. So, his parents decided that he would move in with his dad, Richard, and stepmom, Pat, and attend a private school for his eighth-grade year.

Matt was shocked on his first day at Northwest Christian School at how *nice* everybody was to him. He went to Bible class out of curiosity more than anything else.

Later that same year, his beloved grandfather, Bummer, passed away from lung cancer, having been a smoker for most of his life.

Prior to this, Matt said, there hadn't been a lot of strong spiritual influences or examples in his life. But Bummer's death stirred the hearts of Matt's dad and stepmom to want their kids to have more of a spiritual anchor in their life.

They made a decision that would lead to the most significant moment of Matt's life: they started taking the kids to church.

One night, about six months in, one of the pastors, a man named Jim Forbes, came over to share the gospel with Matt and Jill.

Matt told me how lost he had felt leading up to that night.

From an early age, he had felt the weight of his sin. He was convinced that he deserved God's punishment, so he was baptized in the Catholic church. He thought he was 'safe' after that, but he would still go to bed at night feeling empty, like there was still something missing in his life.

As he talked, I knew just what he was talking about.

When Jim told him that Jesus Christ had died to save him from the wrath of God, that it was simply by believing in Him that he could be saved, he realized that this was what he was missing. He repented and believed in Jesus Christ that night, and after that, he told me, everything was different.

Bible class became instantly more applicable. It was there he learned that Jesus was not just an angel; He was God—a truth which changed Matt's whole view of Who it was that died on the cross for his sin.

He skipped forward and finished by saying that he was currently a software engineer intern hoping to receive a full-time offer of employment and that he liked rock climbing, reading his Bible, going to church, and attending small group.

I was silent as he talked, thinking how different we grew up.

I grew up going to church every Sunday, memorizing verses in AWANA, and going to youth group and church camp. Even with all that, though, my sin had never felt weighty, and everything about church and the Bible had always seemed so forced and boring.

But here was this 23-year-old guy who had not had near the Christian influence I had been privileged to have, and he was reading his Bible every morning and going to church *just because he wanted to.*

I knew right then that this man was holding onto something stronger than a fraying rope.

I had been trying with all my might to find joy and happiness in my frivolity, and, frankly, sin, but it wasn't anywhere to be found. If anything, all I found was more emptiness. But listening to this man, it seemed as though, somehow, joy and happiness had found *him.*

In that moment, I breathed a prayer: "God, I know I haven't been living my life the way I should be. Will you please give me a second chance and just let me marry this guy?"

We chatted about other things on the way back. We ducked into the backyard of his friend's house, jumped on their trampoline (which he assured me was totally fine), borrowed a couple of their skateboards, and skateboarded the rest of the way back to his house. He made me laugh the whole way.

By the end of that night, I was certain of three things.

Matt Dodd was *the* funniest person I knew.

He knew Christ in a way I didn't.

And I wanted to marry him with all my heart.

CHAPTER 2

Use Me, God, for Big Things!

I was someone who was saved because Matt Dodd invited them to church.

It was 5pm on August 1st, 2004, and we were seated in the auditorium of Tempe High School—the temporary home of East Valley Bible Tempe. It was an unusual time to go to church but made necessary because of the needs of the high school.

I looked around at the couple hundred people or so scattered throughout the auditorium and noticed that a majority of them were close to my age, maybe a few years older. Matt had told me the church was originally planted by the college group of a church in Gilbert—hence, the younger demographic.

One of the pastors got up to give a short message before communion, something Matt said they did every Sunday. I sat back, sure that I already knew everything he was going to say.

Except, I didn't.

It's funny how we can say a million words, but all God needs is a single phrase to change a heart.

All that I remember that pastor saying was something I had heard a thousand times before: that on the cross, Jesus bore the wrath we deserved.

But on that night, those words pierced my heart.

The truth of how I had been living became strikingly obvious. I had been living a totally godless life while claiming to know God. Not only did I feel the weight of my sin in that moment, I was crushed by it. That night, I knew without a doubt that I *did* deserve God's wrath. I deserved hell.

I realized that that rope I had been holding onto—the one with the fraying strands—was made up of my own attempts to be "pretty good" before God. No wonder it was failing—there wasn't any goodness in me! That rope couldn't save me; in fact, it only seemed to condemn me the more I held on to it.

Sitting in that auditorium, I looked at what Jesus had done for me on the cross, and I *loved* him for the first time. Here was a rope made up of something stronger; one that would not fray or break or fail; one that would hold onto *me*.

By God's grace, I grabbed hold of eternal life through Jesus Christ. I wouldn't have been able to tell you that night that I had just been saved; I thought I already was. But in the weeks and months following, it was as though my parched soul began tasting water for the first time.

The Bible was a new book to me, alive and convicting. Church was no longer a bore; small group was truly fellowship.

As ASU started back up in August, we got to go to school together; me pursuing the ever-elusive undergraduate degree and Matt, his graduate.

We began meeting at coffee shops most mornings before school to read the Bible together. Matt quickly realized that although I knew a lot of Bible verses, I had no idea what it actually said. In his self-effacing, humble way, he began to help me read the Bible as one book, telling one story of incredibly good news.

Over the next nine months, Matt and I did everything together.

We went to church together, small group together, taught Sunday school together.

We went cliff jumping and rock climbing; we danced in parking lots and spent lots of late nights at IHOP doing our homework, or studying our Bibles together, or hanging out with his friends.

It was Matt's habit as he read his Bible in the morning to write out his prayers in journals.

One of his journal entries from this time reads:

"God, I come before You now, Lord, just asking for You to open my heart and let me see good things from Your word. God, please let me remember You today, and please be real in my life. Don't let me for a second ever think that I can do this on my own, but, God, help me to continually seek Your face, and know You more.

"Help me to be as much of a leader as I can in this relationship. God, use me and help me to see the big picture in life, and use me, God, for big things! God, I ask that I can get into grad school and do well. Help me to serve at church and be a light for those around me, and, God, if you want me on the mission field, please be changing my heart!"

CURLY HAIR AND BRACES

Matt was passionate about missions.

It had started long before he met me by just being involved with ASU campus ministries like Campus Crusade for Christ, organizations which strived to proclaim the gospel on college campuses while also engaging students in super-fun activities. Being super-fun himself, Matt was a magnet for inviting people either to church or to these meetings, and he loved it.

Campus Crusade, Cru for short, would often take students from college campuses all over the nation on short-term mission trips.

In 2001, Matt had gone on one of these mission trips to Santa Cruz, California the summer after his first year of college.

His journals during this time are filled with thanksgiving to God, prayers for good surfing, and a desire to be used by God. One journal entry from this time reads:

"Dear God, thank you for bringing me out to Santa Cruz. I don't think I'll ever understand how big you really are, God. Forgive me for screwing up so much, God! I hate it how I get so caught up in the things of this world that I forget what life is really about. You've brought me through so much, I've been

through so much, it's just crazy, God. To think back on my youth and where I am now, I just want to praise you, Lord.

"God, I'm scared about the future. I know I was like this last year. I had a good and fun year, but not good spiritually. Help me to be a good emcee. I pray that I'll be funny and spur my fellow Christians on to grow closer to You."

He spent the summer working at a coffee cart on the Santa Cruz boardwalk, making himself an Oreo shake every day and giving them away to his friends. He surfed at night with his friends, went cliff jumping, and—most of all—used his gregarious personality to share the gospel with complete strangers.

It was a summer that opened his eyes to how people all over the world needed to hear the gospel and that he could be part of that.

When another Cru trip rolled around the following summer in 2002, Matt signed up to go. But this time it wasn't to the state next door—it was to East Asia.

Matt in East Asia was something to behold.

His 5' 10" frame, wild curly hair and braces didn't exactly blend in with the people there. And then there was the day when all the guys on the mission team went to an Asian hair salon to dye their hair blond, only to have it turn out more of an orange-blond color, making Matt stand out even more.

As always, his exuberant personality matched his new hair.

Since one of Cru's goals that summer was to build relationships with students at the university they attended, Matt went about this in the most ridiculous way he could, telling his new Asian friends things like, "In America, no girls find Josh attractive (another member of the team); they only find me attractive." Or he would be running late to class one day and say, "In America, everyone is ten minutes late."

His joy and humor drew people to him, regardless of the language. Soon, Matt had many new Asian friends, and proceeded to give them all nicknames that rhymed, like Sky, Fly, etc.

Underneath all the silliness, however, Matt took seriously the reason why he was in East Asia. Despite his goofiness in building these relationships, he was able to share the gospel within them.

By the end of the summer, dozens of students expressed a desire to follow Christ. Matt's spiritual growth happened by degrees, and with this trip, the Lord strengthened his desire to see others reached for Christ on a global level.

One journal entry from this time reads:

> *"Dear God, I want to come before you in prayer and supplication for these guys I am talking to, God! I want to pray that You would use me to tell them the gospel, and that they would come to a trust in You—for Sky and Famous, Small Fish and Eric.*
>
> *"God, I think You have been talking to me about living more by Your Spirit, but I've still been "quenching the spirit" when it comes to stepping out in faith and talking to people.*
>
> *"I have much to pray about in the future, God! Whether or not to be an RA or a long-term missionary. I also pray, Lord, for my future wife, that You would continue to bless her relationship with You and sanctify her.*
>
> *"God, help me to become the leader that You desire and I was meant to be! God, I like having fun and being funny, but I still need help just not doing that all the time.*
>
> *"How I long to be in heaven with You, Lord, where I won't have these struggles and I can have perfect worship and fellowship with You!"*

Matt came home from East Asia desiring to go right back.

When I entered the picture, I got to hear all the crazy stories from both summers. I had heard Matt express a desire to return to east Asia someday, but I didn't think he was serious about wanting to be a full-time missionary.

At the time, I had zero desire to be a part of God's plan for the nations as I was just desiring to be a part of God's plan for me. Little did I know what that plan would end up including.

28

Smarter Than My Brief Calculus Homework

Matt and I were friends for an agonizingly long two weeks before we officially began dating. And then, only after he met with my dad and asked permission to date me with the intention of marrying me.

Our semester at ASU continued. We passed notes between classes, filled with silliness and spiritual encouragement. We spent our lunches reading our Bibles, talking about what we had been learning, and making up outlandish nicknames for each other.

Chicken. Goose. Chicken's goose.

Meanwhile, Matt, it turned out, was smart.

I had been so taken in by his unassuming demeanor and goofy mannerisms that I figured he struggled academically like the rest of us. But whenever I would work on my Brief Calculus homework, he would take one look at the problem, tell me the answer, and always be right.

Always.

I realized that in addition to this man being *almost* funnier than me, he was also smarter than my brief calculus homework.

Never one to talk about his achievements, it was only in the writing of this book that I learned that Matt was a National Merit Scholar and came into ASU attending the Barrett Honors College on a full-ride academic scholarship.

He also had a minor in Math.

The International House of Hosting Birthday Parties

About a month after we started dating, Matt's friends threw him a birthday party at IHOP.

IHOP—hosting poor college kids' birthday parties since 1958.

I remember being shocked at how many people showed up at IHOP to celebrate him. One of his friends wrote him a song filled with inside jokes I knew nothing about and sang it to him on his guitar. By the end of the night, I knew two more things about this guy I had only known for two months: he had a lot of friends, and he was *loved* by them.

These friends were not your run-of-the-mill, convenient college attachments. I didn't know it then, but many of the friendships that sat around the table that night had lasted through ASU, Santa Cruz, East Asia. With Jesus as their common denominator, they were friendships that were forged in a lifetime mold.

Over a decade later, upon hearing that Matt was sick, these friends would come from far and wide to be at his side.

COMING TO THE WORD OF GOD
TO KNOW THE GOD OF THE WORD

A significant part of Matt's spiritual growth during this time was the good teaching he was under in his local church.

His pastor would often say, "We come to the Word of God to know the God of the Word." Matt's desire to *know* God was growing. More and more, he was being tethered, not to feelings or experiences, but to the truth of God's Word. One journal entry reads:

"God, please open the eyes of my heart and help me understand Ephesians and let it change my life! God, I desperately need You to show me good things from Your Word because I want to know You more! Please help me be a spiritual leader in all areas of my life and to dwell on You and Your Words."

Quotes from his pastors are sprinkled throughout his journal entries, such as, "Every day, position your heart to hear the word of God." Instead of only prayers scrawled in his beautifully slanted cursive handwriting, there were now Bible passages written out, where Matt was learning to study what the Bible said, and notes from sermons he was hearing.

He began taking a class at church designed to disciple men called BUILD. The goal of the class was to teach biblical priorities for men: first, to care spiritually for their hearts, then their homes, and then their ministries.

The lessons he learned in this class were invaluable, shaping how he led his own heart, home, and ministry for the rest of his life.

SHE-MATT AND THE RING

In Matt's words, I was "pretty cool for a girl" and also pretty funny.

Matt was about 5% funnier than I was up until his last day. But I could hold my own with all of the competitions between his friends to see who was the funniest.

I also worked hard to be just as ridiculous as Matt, except perhaps not as much when it came to animals. Matt was forever putting unsuspecting cats under his shirt or small dogs in his pockets until they jumped or clawed their way out.

It was good for us to have some differences.

Later on, I would learn that they called me She-Matt.

Since Matt lived only a couple blocks from ASU, I would often park at his house and we would walk to school together.

Every morning I would show up with the goal of leaving as soon as possible, since it was evident none of the guys who lived there was going to school for housekeeping. Mold grew in the bathrooms. Unsuspecting cockroaches would suddenly be shot with airsoft gun bullets as they skittered up the wall. There was a tater tot on the floor between the oven and the fridge the first day I walked into that house, and that tater tot was still on the floor the last day I walked into that house.

But every morning when I would show up, there Matt was, on the couch, reading his Bible, writing out his prayers.

Missions began to come up more and more in my conversations with Matt—East Asia in particular—and I began to realize that this was a very real part of this man. I needed to make some serious decisions about what I wanted in my life.

There came a night where Matt and I went out to dinner at a little restaurant on an airport strip, and I realized that I would rather be with this man preaching the gospel in East Asia or wherever else in the world he wanted to go, than live anywhere else without him.

That night I told him and meant it with all my heart, "Matt, I'll follow you anywhere for missions. Even to East Asia."

Unbeknownst to me, he bought the ring the next day.

GLOW STICKS BY THE OCEAN

On January 21, 2005, Matt wrote this in his journal:

> *"Dear God, Lord, I'm so ridiculously excited! I think today was the longest day at work I could have ever had. Lord, please help everything tonight go according to plan! Please God, help/let/allow/equip/enable our relationship to glorify and honor You!! God, You've been so good to me and Cameron and we just don't deserve it! I pray that I can know You more and love You more after tonight, and together with Cameron!*
>
> *"God, I don't know why You've decided to show us grace, but, God, I'm so thankful for it! Please open my eyes so I can see good things from Your word! I pray that I can always be patient with Cameron and show her love and love her like Christ loves the church, giving Himself up for her!"*

There came a night where Matt picked me up from work to take me on a date in his little teal Toyota Tercel.

It had been a long day at work for me, and knowing I was scheduled to work again the next morning, I was looking forward to just a quick date so I could go to bed.

We drove and drove....and *drove*.

After 45 minutes of driving, no amount of rose-colored glasses, starry-eyed feelings of love could stop me from getting annoyed. I was just about to start talking about insensitivity towards other people's sleep schedules when we passed a sign that read: San Diego-280 miles.

Just then, my boss called to let me know that I conveniently no longer had to be at work the next morning.

And I knew.

In the middle of the night, we pulled up to some cliffs next to the ocean.

I was dead tired and hopeful that we were going to take a nap in the car before we did any cliff-side sightseeing, when Matt, full of energy, said, "Let's get out and explore!"

I looked at him because, well, it was *three in the morning*, but got out of the car anyway. Immediately, wind was whipping through my hair and the thunderous sound of crashing waves filled the night air around me. I looked around for Matt.

That's when I saw the glow sticks.

A faint trail of them led up and over the cliffs, toward the breaking waves that I could not see in the darkness. It felt like a dream, stumbling up and over the rocky cliffs, following Matt and the faint glows of green and blue and red and yellow.

I followed the glow sticks until they crested a small hill.

Suddenly, I saw a clearing ahead ablaze with light. Dozens of flickering candles surrounded a table with a cake on it. A video camera was set up nearby, and, as I moved closer, I heard the strains of my favorite song playing from some hidden radio.

Disbelievingly, I sat in one of the chairs at the table and watched as Matt got down on one knee. In the glow of candles and glow sticks, he opened a ring box.

He said kind things to me, that he glorified God more with me in his life than without.

And then, he asked me to marry him.

I said yes.

Whoops and cheers went up from the cliffs all around us, and that's when I saw the small army of friends that loved Matt enough to put all this together in California at three in the morning.

On May 12th, 2005, Matt and I were wed in a small venue in Phoenix.

I walked barefoot down the aisle to a beaming Matt, and we shared our first kiss after we both said 'I do'.

It was a wonderful day, culminating with an epic first dance that Matt and I spent way too many weeks choreographing at my parent's house to a mash-up of our favorite songs.

When Matt had asked my dad official permission to marry me, my dad had only two conditions: that Matt have a stable job and that I finish college.

Fortunately, Matt had just gotten that permanent job offer from his internship that he was hoping for.

And he promised my dad that he would do everything he could to make sure I finished college that year.

He could not, of course, have foreseen the accident that would prevent him from keeping that promise.

CHAPTER 3

Being Mastered by That One Very Great Thing

As we settled into married life in May of 2005, Matt entered the world of corporate America, faithfully spending eight hours a day in a cubicle that was cold and dark.

Literally.

For some reason, his co-workers liked to work only with the light from the skylights in the building and turned the lights off.

For a super enthusiastic, outgoing personality like Matt Dodd, this was a struggle.

He would come home, remember what it was like to talk to people, go to sleep, wake up, and do it all over again. It all felt so futile to him at times.

Years earlier, Matt attended a conference called One Day.

At this conference, a pastor named John Piper pleaded with those in attendance not to waste their lives.

He told a story of a pair of retired women almost eighty years old who were in Cameroon preaching the gospel when they died in a sudden car crash. And then he told another story of an older couple who were retired, playing softball and collecting shells in Florida.

He pleaded with the students at the conference not to waste their lives collecting shells but to spend them for something that would never perish—the gospel!

The words of that preacher not to waste his life reverberated through Matt for the rest of his life. As a software engineer, he struggled to see how he was making his life count for the gospel and longed for something more.

He prayed:

"God, I know that I need You so badly! I don't want to waste my life just being an engineer for the rest of my life. I want to live for You because there is nothing else on this earth I want more than You! I know You have a plan. Is it just for me to wake up, read, go to work, and then do it again? I don't want to go my whole life and just live a mediocre life. I want to be an exceptional husband and father and be bold for the gospel! Can I do that, Lord?"

Piper opened the conference with these words:

"You don't have to know a lot of things in order to make a huge difference for the Lord in the world. But you do need to know a few things that are great and be willing to live for them and die for them. People that make a difference in the world are not people who have mastered a lot of things; they are people who have been mastered by a very few things that are very, very great."

These words stayed with Matt and years later, when he grabbed a small journal to carry with him to trek across the mountains of Papua New Guinea for the sake of the gospel, he would write this quote on its front page.

Matt longed to be mastered by those very few, very great things every morning when he read his Bible. It was this year that Matt's journals begin to reflect a deeper study of God's Word. Studying the beatitudes, Matt wrote:

"Matthew 5:6 – "Blessed are those who hunger and thirst for righteousness, for they shall be satisfied." We hunger and thirst every day because our bodies need food in order to stay alive. The longer we wait, the more we hunger and thirst.

"In the same way, hunger and thirst after righteousness knowing you need righteousness to stay alive. You can't go on without it for long because you will die. It's a necessity in your life to have righteousness. For the righteous shall be satisfied!"

Similarly, when he got to verse ten about persecution, Matt wrote:

"Blessed are those who are persecuted for righteousness' sake, for theirs is the kingdom of heaven." In these beatitudes, this is the last one. "For the sake of righteousness." All the others are kind of things that come from the inside and work themselves out. But this one is saying that it is a natural flow of events then for persecution to come from the outside.

"It's almost like if you are pure in heart, merciful, gentle, peacemakers, mourning over your sin, then you will be righteous, and there is a good chance you will be persecuted. It's funny, too, that these people are peacemakers. Isn't it always the peacemakers who are persecuted? Look at Jesus' life, or even the prophets of the Old Testament. Hebrews 11:35, "and others were tortured, not accepting their release, so that they might obtain a better resurrection; and others experienced mockings and scourging, yes also chains and imprisonment."

"The fact of the matter is there just weren't a lot of people in the Bible who weren't persecuted, if not killed, for their faith."

Matt saw having Christ as better than having anything else on this earth. Written in large letters on one of his journal pages during this year are the words: "Christ + Nothing = Everything!"

One day shortly after we were married, Matt asked me if I would be willing, when we were old and it was looking like it was close to the end, to go to Pakistan or somewhere that was opposed to the gospel, start preaching the gospel in the streets, and let them stone us.

My response at the time was not a high five.

Matt was not in any way suicidal; he lived life more than anyone I knew. But from our first days of being married onward, it was clear that Matt wanted to honor God in his death. His first thought was to do that through persecution or martyrdom, but ultimately, he wanted to do that in whatever way he could. And in the meantime, he was continually striving to be mastered by that One Very Great Thing.

FALLING OFF A CLIFF…LITERALLY

To say we had a tough first year of marriage would be an understatement.

Our plan was to wait a few years before having any kids, but God had a different plan. One that included me falling off a cliff.

Literally.

Matt and I had been married for three months when we drove up with a big group of friends to Payson, Arizona, to hike Box Canyon for the day. What started off as a big group was quickly pared down to Matt, myself, and our friend, Joel, as people went their separate ways.

It rained off and on as we navigated our way along the river at the bottom of the canyon. As we hiked, we would occasionally come to drop-offs where we had to decide if the water below was deep enough to jump in or if we needed to find another way down.

We came to one such cliff, which dropped about twenty-five feet, where there was water on one side and rocks on the other. Matt and Joel went over to check out how deep the water was, and I went over to look at the rock side.

Armed with youthful invincibility, I glanced at the rocks below and was confident I could scale down the cliff.

As it began to sprinkle again, I threw my whole body out on a ledge. My fingers gripped one slippery rock edge while the tips of my wet sneakers perched on another.

Matt glanced over, saw what I was doing, and opened his mouth to call out for me to stop.

It was too late.

I slipped.

Suddenly, I was falling to the rocks below.

As my face scraped the rocks on the way down, I thought, "What a foolish way to die."

My left leg hit first, shattering my ankle into pieces that would later need multiple screws and rods to be put back together, the impact obliterating all the cartilage. My left wrist hit the ground next, knocking diamonds out of my new wedding ring.

In God's kindness, my head struck last.

While I never lost consciousness, the impact knocked the wind out of me violently, and, for about a minute, I couldn't move or breathe.

Seeing my body crumpled and motionless on the rocks below, Matt assumed the worst.

"Go, get help!" he yelled to Joel.

Joel immediately hiked out of the canyon alone. With no cell phone, he made it to the road, flagged down a car, and called 911.

Back in the canyon, I eventually got my wind back.

I sat up, took one look at my compound-fractured ankle, blood trickling down the side, and screamed. I put my hands on the ground behind me to scoot myself back, only to have my broken wrist collapse, and screamed again.

Matt exhaled in relief.

"Hold on!" he called.

It was still raining, and I had just fallen off this cliff, but Matt—being Matt—wasted no time.

He took his shoes off, threw them down to me, and then proceeded to scale barefoot the very rock face I had just fallen off.

He dragged me under a ledge to get me out of the rain, and we waited, not knowing if Joel had made it out; not knowing if help would come.

Three long hours later, a volunteer search-and-rescue team found us. They assembled a rope-and-pulley system that stretched down all six hundred feet into the canyon. I was duct-taped into a stretcher and hauled up, sometimes hanging vertically, out of the canyon.

During one of the moments where I hung suspended in mid-air, hundreds of feet of canyon below me, concerned about being dropped, our friend, Nate, helpfully said, "Cameron, you just fell. It's statistically unlikely for anyone else to fall today."

Eventually, I reached the top where I was whisked to a hospital.

The ankle fracture was severe. While several surgeries would piece it back together and allow me to walk again, the fall effectively removed all the cartilage in my ankle joint, rendering me arthritic at the age of 21.

With my ankle and wrist injuries combined, I would be in a wheelchair for the next three months.

These were trying circumstances.

And then we got pregnant.

PRESSING ON TO KNOW THE LORD

Matt went from being a single guy, to a husband, a caretaker, and a father in the span of four months. Because of the limits of what I could do for myself, my grandparents graciously moved in with us so Matt could go to work.

Between the stress of the injury and the busyness of having houseguests, Matt and I began to slack in our Bible reading. Almost immediately, through the unattended spiritual gaps and cracks in our hearts, sin crept in.

When sin was finally confessed, the inevitable fall-out was painful and culminated in some ugly quarrels.

But that rope to which we both clung held fast to us.

Matt knew his sin was first and most before God, and, while my heart was embittered towards him, Matt sought solace in the Lord:

December 10, 2005

"Matthew 8 throughout the chapter. A lot of times what we see is Christ just healing people. Everyone came to Him and He healed them, yet none of them deserved it. The people that drew closest to Christ were those that were desperate, hurting sinners and Christ healed them because these people knew that they needed help and their problems were too big for anyone else on earth to solve.

"And what's more is Christ drew near to them and healed them! God, please give me the faith to draw near to You every day as a desperate sinner. Please heal

me, Lord. If you can heal the sick, dying, and wounded, then I know that You can heal me!"

"Please help Cameron to forgive me! Please heal and mend our relationship. It's good to be with You again, though, God. Isaiah 30:18-20, 'Therefore the Lord waits to be gracious to You, and therefore He exalts Himself to show mercy to You...' God, thank You for Your grace! I don't deserve anything You've given me! God, if You take everything away tomorrow, as long as I have You, I'll be okay!"

Matt was a leader in our marriage and repentance was no different. When there was a conflict between us, he was the first to humble himself and apologize.

In the midst of this conflict, we were broken people—one of us quite literally—and we could not bind ourselves.

The banner that flew over our marriage that year was Hosea 6:1, 3: "Come, let us return to the Lord; for He has torn us, that He may heal us; He has struck us down, and He will bind us up...Let us know; let us press on to know the Lord; His going out is as sure as the dawn; He will come to us as the showers, as the spring rains that water the earth."

We knew how we had ended up here.

We had stopped reading our Bibles; we had stopped pressing on to know the Lord.

Yes, our circumstances were difficult. I was in a wheelchair, unable to even go to the bathroom by myself, for three months. Matt was working forty hours a week while trying to care for his disabled and pregnant wife.

But at the end of the day, the only place where hope for difficulty is found—be it physical trauma or emotional—was in God's Word! And we had neglected to remind ourselves of this.

The lesson we learned that year was that we can never stop reading our Bibles, *especially* in trials! God was so kind to teach us this lesson early in our marriage because, in so doing, He grew us in ways which we never would have grown otherwise.

We learned this lesson the hard way.

But we never forgot it.

Years later, when one of us would again be in a wheelchair, we would remember the lesson we learned this very first year.

The damage to my ankle was permanent; I would have severe arthritis in my ankle for the rest of my life, limiting my mobility and causing constant low-level pain.

But the lessons we learned were just as permanent and of far more value than two good ankles or a smooth first year of marriage.

CHAPTER 4

Do You Know For Sure You *Don't* Want to Go to Papua New Guinea?

O n June 16, 2006, we welcomed Susanna Joy Dodd into the world. With Susanna, we began our tradition of naming our kids based off of where we were reading the Bible, as well as giving them all fruit of the Spirit middle names.

Our pastor was preaching through Luke 8 when we were pregnant and so Susanna was her name.

That first year of parenthood was filled with new experiences: having a baby with colic, figuring out how to change diapers and be *anywhere* on time, and getting a golden retriever named Bodhi, who ate everything.

We went to church and small group, but Matt still struggled to find meaning in the cubicle life. He wasn't sure what he was supposed to be doing with his life. All he knew was that he didn't want to waste it, and his prayers during this time reflect that:

"God, please don't let me live the ordinary American life. How I long to have a full life and to be used big in Your kingdom to reach the lost. Either way, God, I pray that we don't live average lives and we don't have a mediocre relationship with You all our lives, but that we would be living missional lives now! God, I know this life is short and I don't want to waste it!"

"God, You know my heart. I just don't know what I'm supposed to be doing with my life, especially at work. But God, until I hear from You, I'm just

going to be diligent and holy, honest and set apart. And God, I also ask that I would be bold with the gospel and spread truth in the workplace!"

The time Matt spent living the 'ordinary American life', being diligent and holy, wasn't wasted.

God was growing Matt in his knowledge of Him, in personal godliness, in being a missionary in that cold, dark cubicle. Growing him through every day Bible reading like the following:

"Psalm 128:4 – 'Behold, thus shall the man be blessed who fears the Lord'. I know that fearing the Lord is noticed the most when there is a situation and there is something else to fear—the fear of man, fear of rejection—then all of a sudden, there is no fear of the Lord. God, I pray I can fear You always. Please give me courage and boldness!"

The Lord was also teaching Matt how to wait on Him and be patient and trust.

"God, I know Your timing is not always what we think. Please help me to wait on You, to be steadfast, even if things never change in my life; that I would hope in You and trust in Your goodness. Surely, You were good to Job and Paul and Abraham and Joseph and Joshua. Please, God, help me to be patient because I believe You are working all things out for the good of those who believe! And let me consider this quote by Charles Simeon:

'Infinite wisdom has arranged the whole with infinite love; and infinite power enables me to rest upon that love. I am in a dear Father's hands-all is secure. When I look to Him, I see nothing but faithfulness and immutability and truth; and I have the sweetest peace. I cannot have more peace.' Father, let this be my heart all the days of my life."

In 2006, we attended a conference called Resolved together where John Piper spoke on Philippians 1:20-21, "as it is my eager expectation and hope that I will not be at all ashamed, but that with full courage now as always Christ will be honored in my body, whether by life or by death. For to me to live is Christ, and to die is gain."

Matt's notes record this:

> *"Paul's passion is that his life and death will make Jesus look good. How do you die in a way to make Jesus look good? Verse 21, "to die is gain". To breathe the last breath with the confidence that this moment is gain, even though at that moment you are losing everything!"*

Missions had taken a backseat in our marital conversations, overshadowed by the cliff accident, as well as having a baby.

But July of 2007 brought it up again.

One of Matt's good friends from high school, Josh Ruyle, came to town. Josh had gone on both Crusade trips with Matt to Santa Cruz and East Asia and had actually gone back to East Asia for a longer term. He and his wife had just finished a two-year stint over there and came over for dinner.

In the course of that conversation, they asked us where we were at with missions. Matt and I laughed it off, saying that maybe we would go somewhere one day, if that's what God called us to do.

"Well, what are you waiting for?" Josh asked. "An angel to come down from heaven to tell you to go? Isn't that what the Great Commission already said?"

Matt and I woke up the next morning with both of our hearts convicted. We decided that if there was somewhere that needed the gospel and we were able to go, we should at least attempt it.

We began reading the book *Operation World*, which lists all the countries in the world alongside their need for the gospel.

We were overwhelmed.

Finding a place to go felt like finding a needle in an earth-shaped haystack. But we talked to our pastors, kept doing research, and prayed.

We couldn't see then the small village in the rugged mountains with its two waterfalls. Didn't yet know the names and faces of the people who would become so dear to us.

But we knew that we were following the One who knew all of those things and trusted Him to lead us exactly where we were supposed to go.

DO YOU KNOW FOR SURE YOU *DON'T* WANT TO GO TO PAPUA NEW GUINEA?

As we looked into different options for missions, (and had another baby—Benaiah Peace Dodd, born October of 2007), we heard about a week-long seminar held by Wycliffe Bible Translators about Bible translation.

Off we went in June of 2008 to Idyllwild, California with our two little kids in tow.

It was here that we heard for the first time that there were still languages in the world that not only didn't have the Bible—in fact, they weren't even written down yet!

Matt's heart was gripped by Romans 10:14, "How then will they call on him in whom they have not believed? And how are they to believe in him of whom they have never heard? And how are they to hear without a preacher?"

We came home from that seminar willing to go so that a people might no longer be without a preacher.

Matt prayed about the uncertainty of the future like this:

"Father, good morning! God, I'm so fearful about the future. I don't know what will happen with my job or with missions for us, but oh God, I want to trust You! I don't think I should do missions because it sounds cool and then I won't be away from my family, but I want to do it to honor and glorify You!

"Father, You are good and You have been faithful in the past. You saved me and worked in me throughout high school. You brought me to ASU and gave me wonderful, godly friends. You brought me to Santa Cruz, East Asia, and Cameron! Now I trust You will continue to work and be good! Only let me believe it, God!"

Bible translation to an unreached people was now the goal…but where? In what language?

One of Matt's longtime friends, Cass, put us in contact with two missionaries named Joey and Brooke Tartaglia who were home on furlough from the country of Papua New Guinea. They had a heart for the languages around them where no one was yet working and wanted to train people while they were in the States to go.

Papua New Guinea, we soon learned, was an island north of Australia. Though only the size of Texas, it held over 10% of all the world's languages—over 800 languages! The reason for this kind of linguistic diversity was its rugged terrain.

Steep mountains covered in dense rainforest, fast-flowing rivers, earthquakes, landslides, swamps, volcanos. There might be two language groups only a few miles away from each other as the crow flies, and yet never really interact because of the topographical obstacles in between.

Because of their remote location, the majority of these languages had no Scripture and were not even written down.

Having laid out the clear need for someone to go to this place and heard our desire to go somewhere, Joey asked, "Do you know for sure that you *don't* want to go to Papua New Guinea?"

Of course we couldn't say that.

Interested enough to give training with Joey a shot, we met with him every week for the next eight months to learn what planting a church in a village in Papua New Guinea—PNG, for short—would look like.

It would not be easy.

We would first need to learn PNG's trade language of Tok Pisin. Then survey villages by helicopter to see if one was willing to invite us in. Then, houses would need to be built, the language would need to be learned…and written down…and a literacy program developed. Finally, the Bible would need to be translated and *then* the gospel of Jesus Christ could be preached.

Even though the task was daunting, the more we heard, the more excited Matt and I became. To be able to bring the gospel that had so radically transformed our own lives to a people who had never heard it was gripping.

With our hearts now set on PNG, we knew we would need training and a team. We thought we would maybe be ready in three years.

We were wrong.

It would end up taking a total of seven years, one pastoral internship, and two semesters of school before we would make it to PNG.

But make it we would, in God's perfect timing.

BECOMING THAT *KIND* OF MAN

Matt and I knew we would need some sort of training before we went off to learn an unwritten language and write it down, but we knew that being spiritually equipped was just as important as being practically equipped.

It was to this end that Matt read his Bible, met regularly with older men, went to discipleship classes, and eventually became a small group leader. He knew he needed to be a qualified man.

Years before, when Matt was getting ready to finish his summer in East Asia, the team that was stationed there full-time asked everyone on Matt's team to pray about possibly coming back that fall for a longer term.

It was a serious plea and it did not fall on deaf ears.

On their way back to the US, Matt shared a room with his friend, Swanny. The trip had already shaped all of their lives in a profound way and together, the two talked over the possibility of returning.

That night, Matt and Swanny talked through all of the obstacles that would come with being the ones to return to East Asia in the fall and they prayed about it.

Then, to each other that night, they both made a commitment to return.

Matt returned to the States with a heart on fire for missions—specifically missions in East Asia—and began talking to his friends and pastors at church.

But when he told his close friend, Jake, about it, he was met with hesitation.

Where Matt saw adventure and evangelism and discipleship, Jake saw red flags. He asked Matt a few important questions:

"Matt, are you right now the *kind* of man who should be going to the other side of the world? Are you the kind of man who confidently knows how to handle Scripture in order to teach and lead others? Is your character where it should be to be an example to those you would want to disciple? Are you *that* kind of man?"

Matt, not expecting these concerns, had a hard time hearing them. But he thought about what he said.

He went from being certain about returning to re-thinking that decision completely. He knew in his heart that his character was not yet what it ought to be in order to model Christ-likeness for others.

And so, when August rolled around and the plane to East Asia took off, only one of the men who made that commitment in that hotel room that night was on it.

Swanny went back for a year.

Matt did not.

Matt would never get the chance to return to East Asia but love for that country would remain deeply embedded in him for the rest of his life.

This was one of the hardest decisions Matt had made in his life up until this point, but it was the right one. And he was only able to make it because God gave him the grace to humble himself under wise counsel—something he would do over and over again.

Matt had been trying to be that *kind* of man ever since that conversation with Jake. He wanted to lead us to be the *kind* of people who should go to Papua New Guinea and was constantly looking for ways to grow us in that regard.

He also read books.

Lots and lots of books.

For someone who would never have professed to be a great reader, Matt read an awful lot of books. Biographies, systematic theologies, Greek and Hebrew textbooks, books on parenting, theology, marriage—over our twelve years together, Matt would read, underline, and make indelible marks on the pages of these books even as they did the same on him.

But while he may have had some ideas on how we could grow spiritually, God had better ones—including the trial we were about to face.

CHAPTER 5

This is Your Will?

In December of 2008, we found out that we were pregnant with our third baby.

We were thrilled and eagerly went to our first OBGYN visit together.

From day one, Matt and I were committed to doing everything we possibly could together—to an almost ridiculous degree. We went to each other's doctor's appointments, no matter how awkward (think: Matt being checked for moles *everywhere* or every OBGYN appointment in existence).

So we were together as we waited eagerly for that amazing moment we had experienced twice before where we would hear our baby's heartbeat for the first time.

But that moment never came.

We could *see* the baby on the monitor, but there was no flurry of a heartbeat, no rapid sounds of a pulse.

It was just…silence.

After two healthy and problem-free pregnancies, we were unprepared for this. Suddenly, we had to come to grips with whether or not we actually believed all of the things we said we believed about God.

Was He still good though our baby died?

Was He still sovereign?

Could we trust Him? Matt wrote:

"Dear God, yesterday, we went to the doctor and found out that our child had no heartbeat. God, I didn't have the joy of the Lord for most of yesterday. I didn't believe a lot of the good things that Your Word told me.

"I didn't prepare my heart like Job. I asked a lot of 'why' questions like why could this happen? I thought a lot about what could have been and it made me sad. God, You haven't changed. You aren't standing aloof in all of this, but You are near, though I may not feel it.

"Please Lord Jesus, comfort my heart and give me trust. O, what painful effects sin has."

Matt had recently led our small group through the book of Job.

What he had taught us from it was that Job did not wake up the morning he lost everything and decide that day to start trusting God with all he had.

He had been in the habit of trusting God with all he had for a long time. So, when the time came and he lost it all, his first reaction was worship, not questioning.

Matt wanted to be like that, but on the day of our miscarriage, he had found that his heart was not prepared to lose that which God had given him.

That night, Matt and I both wrestled with the sorrow of losing our baby and wept together. Matt wrote that night:

1/21/2009   8:30pm

"We talked about saying goodbye to our baby, God. I never thought I would be saying goodbye to someone we don't know. This home feels so empty; it's missing something, another life…this is Your will?"

We acknowledged that night that our baby was still life that God had breathed—even if it was only life breathed for nine weeks. In keeping with our tradition, we decided to name our baby Noah Goodness Dodd.

WHEN THE SMOKE CLEARS, I REALIZE YOU WERE ALWAYS THERE

The next day, we spent a long time in the hospital waiting for surgery, as it was delayed for most of the day.

Matt continued to struggle as I listened to worship music and tried to sleep:

"Dear God, we're still in the hospital and it's about 4pm…not sure if this is going to happen. I keep thinking that perhaps You are waiting because You are going to breathe life into this baby.

"God, I don't know why all these things happen, but please comfort Cameron. God, as I look at her laying, sleeping, carrying Noah, I'm so in love with her, for the joy You've put in her in the midst of tragedy. Please God, heal my wife, bring more children to us, but not what I will, but what You will.

"And here it seems we sit in time, waiting for the distant future to come where we will preach the gospel to people on the other side of the world. How we get there from here, I don't know. Please God, continue to be our Shepherd. May we continue to hear Your voice and follow and please don't lose us!"

The surgery did eventually happen and in the waiting room, Matt's faith, tested by this miscarriage, grew a little stronger as he drew near to the Lord in his sorrow:

"God, I sit here in the waiting room. Noah is gone, but You are still here. God You brought Psalm 30 to me, and though I think that David's prayer came from a life filled with many more downs, this prayer can be my own: "O Lord my God, I cried to You for help, and You have healed me". God, I do feel comforted now and not alone.

"It was hard to see before, but when the smoke clears and I regain my sight, I realize You were always there. "Weeping may tarry for the night, but joy comes with the morning." I think David means You're always faithful.

*"We did weep last night, God, You saw it all. But You have filled me with joy. Thank You for **You,** God. Thank You for being my Shepherd, my Lord, my God.*

"God, give us a love that, though we were to lose everything, we would have You always. God, thank You for Noah Goodness Dodd. It was Your goodness that gave him to us and Your goodness that took him away. This hospital seems so empty, but I don't feel alone. Please comfort Cameron. She once had our baby close; may You be even closer.

"'Sing praises to the Lord, O you his saints, and give thanks to His holy name. For His anger is but for a moment, and His favor is for a lifetime'. O, how Your favor is for a lifetime...yet it doesn't stop then. Across the hall, we've delivered two kids, and now, less than 100 yards away, a third has come and gone. God, may we praise You for Your favor in this life."

We had a small service with my family to honor Noah's little life and Matt wrote out the following for it:

"Noah Goodness Dodd. November-January 22, 2009.

"The Lord is good in giving us Noah for these nine weeks, and He is good in taking him away. We praise and thank God for the morning sickness, for plans, for the joy. We praise and thank God for Noah's presence, for the giving of gifts, and for being able to see him when we did, silent in the womb.

"We hope to see him again someday, but more than that, we hope to see our Lord and Savior Jesus Christ, who died so we might have life."

Having never read Matt's journals prior to the writing of this book, these internal struggles were new for me to read.

But all I could think as I wrote this last section is *praise God.*

Praise God that He is kind and gracious to give us smaller trials to prepare us for bigger ones.

Praise God that Matt was able to see God prove Himself faithful and remain with him as he wavered, doubted, and wondered in one trial so that one day, years later, in a much greater trial, he wouldn't need to do any of those things.

He wouldn't have any questions for His Savior that day because He had already gotten to ask them in the days and years leading up to it.

In the cliff accident, we had gotten to see that rope of God's faithfulness hold fast to us in the midst of our sin and marital struggles.

Now, we got to feel it securely holding us in the buffeting winds of death and loss.

Once again, as the gusts blew harder in our grief, they only seemed to demonstrate that ours was an unbreakable rope—something stronger than our circumstances yet again.

POOR ONESIMUS

In view of the missionary task ahead of us, Matt and I attended the Summer Institute of Linguistics for the first time in in British Columbia in the summer of 2009. We began learning how to hear different sounds, write them down, and develop an alphabet for an unwritten language.

Oh, Canada.

When we weren't in school, we were digging strawberries out of the dirt or camping in Whistler or exploring the city of Vancouver. We watched the sun set at 10:30 at night and saw it come up again just a few hours later.

We also learned to appreciate the metric system.

Sort of.

My mom began what would become a regular habit of hers, visiting us wherever we went in the world.

We learned a massive amount about language in those nine weeks and came back to Phoenix feeling more equipped than ever to pursue Bible translation.

Getting pregnant after a miscarriage is one of the sweetest and most anxiety-inducing gifts God can give.

We had gotten to see God's faithfulness in our miscarriage; so much so, that we knew that regardless of what would happen, He would still be faithful, He would still be good. And yet, trust was needed.

Matt prayed about the pregnancy like this:

"Oh Lord, You are good and You gave us another baby! God, may we cast our anxieties on You about our baby. God, You got us pregnant, please keep us pregnant! May we trust You, and please God, grow the baby if it's Your will. God, I know You will be good and do good no matter what happens! Please, Lord, may we trust You."

In God's kindness, God did grow that baby until he was born Onesimus Faithful Dodd in July of 2010.

Poor Onesimus.

We were reading the book of Philemon at the time, and I so loved the story of the slave who was set free by the gospel that I asked Matt if we could name him Onesimus, but in so doing, we also gave him an uphill battle in terms of people hearing his name right or pronouncing it correctly or just understanding it in general.

On the upside, he is able to read the whole story of his name in the Bible in just twenty-five verses.

And to make life easier, he just tells people to call him Ness.

WHEN QUITTING IS MOVING FORWARD

As 2011 opened, Matt officially moved to part-time as a software engineer in order to spend more time training for the mission field.

We took Greek and Hebrew classes together through the seminary at our church and made plans to attend a second summer at the linguistic program in Canada. Our pastors also invited Matt to be a pastoral intern.

Matt prayed:

"God, it's April 4, 2011. God, I'm excited about things. Going to SIL, filling out the elder application, reading Your word, but God, there are things I'm concerned about, like how is everything going to work out?

"I'd love to go, God, really anywhere! Anywhere there are lost, dying souls! Please send us out, God!

"Please may we be qualified, with qualified people to go with us! God, make me into a man like Paul, able to spend and be spent for the souls of others!

"Oh God, may I especially spend and be spent for my wife and kids before everything else! God, please send us to PNG, or some other place so we can teach others Your word! God, please grow me as a shepherd! Please God, give me wisdom with studying Your word—may I be satisfied in You!"

As we prepared to leave for our second summer of linguistics training, we hit a roadblock with Matt's job.

The first time we had gone to Canada for the summer, Matt's employer had granted him a leave of absence. But the economy in 2011 was not nearly as strong as it had been in 2009 and so we had a difficult decision to make.

In order to move forward with taking the gospel to the nations, Matt would have to quit his job and trust the Lord to provide another job that would allow him to be just as flexible with his working hours when we got back.

He decided to quit.

Off we went to Canada for the second time, this time with three kids in tow.

It was much colder and rainier this time around, with not as many berries and a more intense workload, but it was still a productive and sweet time as a family.

We drove back to Phoenix better equipped linguistically, but without a job for Matt.

At that moment, the future was full of unknowns.

Matt was jobless.

Our plan had always been to go to PNG with teammates and at the moment we had none.

We also had no sending organization to help us get there.

Joey Tartaglia, the missionary who had trained us, had begun the process of starting his own organization, something he called Finisterre Vision, after a mountain range in Papua New Guinea.

The dream was that it might one day become a full-fledged sending organization that would provide infrastructure for missionaries while leaving the leadership and decision-making in the hands of their pastors and local church back home.

This was exactly the kind of organization for which we were searching, but there was a problem.

The dream of Finisterre Vision was just that: a dream.

Even if all the paperwork went through, we would be the first team sent out by it. Meaning, we would have to build all of the infrastructure from the ground up.

So, we kept looking for another option, but we hung on to the dream of Finisterre Vision.

As we drove along the Pacific Coast Highway in California back to Arizona, marveling at the breadth of the ocean and discussing the island that lay far on its other side, we had no answers for any of these things.

But we prayed and trusted and made plans.

And then Matt's phone rang.

TEAM PNG

It was a former co-worker calling, offering to help Matt get a job he had just heard about.

The job ended up being a perfect fit—even allowing him to continue working part-time so he could continue his Greek and Hebrew classes.

Back to the cubicle he faithfully went, still waiting for the day where his job could include breathing fresh air.

Not long after that, our friend, Cass, who had moved on to the greener pastures of marriage, reached out to us with her husband, Zach Cann.

They were seriously considering going with us to PNG.

Suddenly the idea of God providing qualified teammates to go with us to PNG became very concrete.

Matt had a job, we potentially had teammates, and every day that went by, Finisterre Vision looked more and more like the best option. But if we were to go with Finisterre Vision, we would need another family to come and help with logistics, to be the infrastructure we would need in the village.

Our pastors set aside one Sunday in the summer of 2012 to talk about missions and asked if anyone in our church body would be willing to be our logistics coordinators.

In God's providence, Jeremy and Lorie Lehman answered that call.

Though we didn't know them very well at the time, the Lord knew how perfectly suited to this position they would be.

As a team, Zach and Cass Cann (along with their two kids), Jeremy and Lorie Lehman (along with their three kids), and ourselves (with our soon-to-be four kids—surprise! We were pregnant again!) began to talk through what it would look like for us to go to Papua New Guinea together as one, big, fifteen-person family.

Just like that, Team PNG was formed.

We wrapped up the year of 2012 with Mary Love Dodd being born—the easiest name of all our kids (Luke 1:46-55).

She was our fourth kid and would also be our last.

With teammates by our side and a sending organization materializing before our eyes, we began raising support.

This was, by far, the biggest surprise blessing of the whole missionary process.

We got to visit church after church and see the body of Christ do what it does best—love one another and send people out.

We had been walking towards the mission field so slowly for so long, it was hard to believe how much momentum was starting to gather, but with each day that passed, the steps that were taken felt a whole lot more like leaps towards PNG.

We didn't know it, but as New Year's Day greeted us in January of 2014, it would be the year where all of our plans would finally be put into action.

It would be the year we would go to Papua New Guinea.

NOT SITTING IN THE BEST SEATS OR WEARING THE BEST ROBES

As we began to make big decisions together—decisions about life and finances—we soon discovered that we were three very different families in regard to how we viewed our time and finances.

We also learned that we were all sinners.

It was difficult to agree on how we should do things and often brought us into conflict with each other. Yet we pressed on, confident that the God who had saved us could help us love each other even in the midst of disagreements.

Matt fought, as he would throughout our whole time in PNG, to be a peacemaker.

God had indeed been growing him into the *kind* of man who should go to the mission field, the kind of man who would be able to lead by example.

In regard to our team conflict, he wrote:

"God, please help us. We have 6 days left. Please help us to finish packing. God, please may we love Jeremy and Lorie, and Zach and Cass. God, please may we be brothers and sisters. May no root of bitterness or selfish ambition come between us, but instead I ask that we would be selfless, and love our neighbors as ourselves!

"God, I don't know all my heart's desires and motivations, but I'm sure there are desires to sit in the best seats and wear the best robes. God, please purge those sins. Please use us still to bring the gospel to the nations!"

As soon as our work permits were approved, we purchased plane tickets and set our departure date for November 30th, 2014.

Matt wrote this to our supporters as the time of our departure drew near:

"We know that life is short and lives are at stake. People live and die in the jungles of Papua New Guinea without ever knowing the one, true God. We go because of our Savior, because He saved us from our sins, from the wrath that we deserve, and because we want to tell others about the riches of His immeasurable grace!"

Ready or not, the time wound down, and one Sunday morning, our church sent us off. That afternoon, all fifteen of us said goodbye to our families, boarded a plane at Sky Harbor International airport, and were off.

The next two years would be filled with external obstacles, internal struggles, and unforgettably wonderful memories as a family.

They would also be the last two years of Matt's life.

But if Matt could have chosen any way to spend those years, it would have been doing just this: laboring to preach the gospel so that an unreached people might no longer be without a preacher.

Matt with mom, Teresa, and sister, Jill

(From left): Blake, George, and Matt—all three brothers.

Matt working at the coffee cart on the Santa Cruz boardwalk.

Matt in East Asia with his new friends and ridiculous hair.

Matt and Cameron on their wedding day.

(from left: Matt's dad, Richard, Matt, and Mary)

Matt with Bodhi, our beloved golden retriever.

Matt, Cameron, with kids Susanna, Benaiah, and Onesimus in Canada for linguistics school.

CHAPTER 6

Five Planes and Eight Days Later

It took us five planes and eight days, but on December 7th, 2014, after seven years of planning and training, we arrived in Papua New Guinea.

The aircraft got smaller at every leg until we eventually descended stairs to the tarmac at the Madang airport. It consisted of a simple airstrip and a building which resembled a long one-story house.

Stepping off the airplane, we were immediately enveloped in a wave of heat and humidity and new smells. Sitting near the equator, Madang hovers around 90 degrees Fahrenheit and 80% humidity year-round.

Our luggage was unloaded onto a wooden table about a hundred feet from the airplane. We were greeted by some very kind SIL folks (Summer Institute of Linguistics, another mission organization in Papua New Guinea). Doing our best to corral both luggage and children, we were taken to our temporary housing at the SIL compound.

Driving to the compound, I watched the new scenery out the window of the large 12-passenger van. The roads in Madang were mostly dirt, pockmarked with an ever-changing chess board of potholes. We drove past large trash heaps in the middle of town, frequently weaving through stray dogs and pedestrians.

Lack of infrastructure aside, Madang was an undeniably beautiful place. There was a raw splendor in this place and its people.

Beauty and danger seemed to co-exist peacefully here—from the actively swaying palm trees to the deceptively sharp coral beaches. There were the wild, ridiculously close thunderstorms and the free-falling (and dangerous!) coconuts. Malaria and typhoid and tuberculosis were staggering threats here, but the ocean and clouds and mountains were just as staggering. The resting face of the nationals was fierce, but all it took was one smile to transform their countenance to a beaming beacon of joy.

And the colors! From the untamed foliage of the flora and fauna of this tropical island to the brightly dyed blouses, dresses, and 'bilums' (carrying bags used by both men and women) in the market, Madang was colorful even in the hottest of weather.

Adjustments had to be made to thrive in this country, of course.

We learned to adapt to the equatorial heat and near-constant humidity without air-conditioning, as well as an inconsistent power grid.

Translation: we learned to adapt to being sweaty.

All. The. Time.

We became accustomed to the acrid smells of town, from the occasional smoke wafting through our house, to people near us burning trash, to the general lack of deodorant. We learned how to use bleach to disinfect the vegetables we bought from the market and the drinking water from our water tank.

We discovered that roosters crowing only at dawn was a myth—they crow whenever they want, even two in the morning. We learned to compost our food scraps and burn the rest of our trash like everybody else. Making food from scratch was surprisingly arduous coming from the land of convenience meals and take out.

Bit by bit, the unknown became the familiar, and soon we were walking down these streets with more joy than trepidation.

We grew used to the red-stained teeth of our new acquaintances (from the betelnut they constantly chewed—a stimulant in Papua New Guinea similar to chewing tobacco). There was the sweet predictability of the Papua New Guinean ladies at the market fawning over our little ones with their smooth baby feet and fine hair, and the appreciation for a culture where friends holding hands throughout an entire conversation is the norm.

We began learning Tok Pisin—that simple trade language that bridges the other 800 indigenous languages in the country. Within just a few months, we had enough of it grasped to start planning surveys of villages.

PLEASE MAY THIS NOT BE A HILL THAT IS IMPOSSIBLE TO PASS!

We continued to navigate issues as a team.

In addition to the heat and stresses and discomfort that came with living in this new place, we had originally been sent to PNG with one, large "team fund" that we all drew from. As you can imagine, sharing finances with people you're not married to was difficult.

The success of mission work comes down not to tasks or activities, but to the hearts of those involved in it.

A couple of months after we arrived, Matt wrote this:

1/22/2015

"God, it's 11pm Tuesday night. I feel bad. There is conflict in the team, and part of me wants to be defensive about it. Please, God, I pray we would resolve our conflict, and be able to reconcile our relationships. Please, God, help me to love Zach. If there is anything that causes our brother to stumble, please may we help them, and please may we examine our own hearts, God. Please may we not go to bed angry with our brother. God, You are so kind and patient toward us sinners. Please help me help us to love our brother.

"The biggest hills we have crossed over, God. Oh, please, may this not be a hill that is impossible to pass. If it means the gospel going to a tribe who has never heard it, then we can change the way we spend our money, the way we spend our time. These things are so small in the grand scheme of things! Please may nothing get in the way of us accomplishing the gospel mission."

It became clear that if we were to fail as a team, it would not be because of external conflicts and obstacles (of which there were many!), but those inside. The years Matt spent wondering what he was doing with his life, God was slowly, incrementally growing him into the kind of man who could think rightly about just such a situation.

Gone were the journal entries of wondering about future usefulness and leisurely Bible study. From this point forward, Matt's journal entries reflect cries and pleas for help with each new struggle, within our team and outside of it.

"God, thank you that we are here with Cass and Zach and Jeremy and Lorie. What a good team You have put together. Please, God, keep us from bitterness or envy or jealousy or strife.

"God, we have left our homes, and our families, and the "conveniences" of life in the US. But that alone doesn't make us holy. God, please make us holy here. Please may this time be a time where we can grow so much in trusting You and knowing You! I do ask, God, that You would grow us here…that we would come back totally changed people, that we would be able to go back to America as if we have gone to seminary.

"For so long, God, I prayed that You would use us in Papua New Guinea—that if it was Your will we could go. And now here we are. We are here! And I'm praying the same thing! God, please use us here. Please help us to find the pocket of people that don't know You…please may there be a tribe out there where we can learn their language and preach the gospel!"

Despite the challenges on our team, progress continued in language learning and other sweet memories were made.

We celebrated our first Thanksgiving in Papua New Guinea as a team.

Shockingly, there was a frozen Butterball turkey in the Madang grocery store freezer.

Just one.

One lonely, suspicious-looking Butterball turkey that looked like this wasn't its first Thanksgiving in that freezer. Or its second.

We opted for duck instead and had a lovely duck Thanksgiving team dinner.

We got to experience remarkably intense thunderstorms together, waited out the frequent power outages together, persevered each time our kids got sick together, and watched the Lord overcome obstacle after obstacle together—be it financial, logistical, or spiritual.

We were struggling, but we were struggling together.

As brothers and sisters in Christ, we were still united in this gospel work, with each of us literally pouring our blood, sweat, and tears into it.

We were weak and we were weary, but we knew the One who gives power to the faint and increases strength to him who has no might, so we trusted Him and stayed the course.

SURVEY SAYS!

There are hundreds of villages in the Finisterre Mountain range of Papua New Guinea, and most of them are extremely hard to reach.

Unless you own a dinghy.

Or a helicopter.

Ideally, both.

Or you love to hike through arguably the toughest terrain on the planet.

Unfortunately for us, we had none of the above.

Oh sure, Matt was all about the adventure of hiking through the jungle at first.

From that first run up A-mountain on that hot July night, I knew I didn't stand a chance of being more active than Matt. The man was always doing something to stay in shape—push-ups, pull-ups, rock climbing, yoga, wrestling mightily with golden retrievers and small children.

We're talking about someone who, when we would go to Disneyland as a family, would get excited because he saw it as *exercise*.

One time, we were staying at a hotel near the park, and while waiting in the Will-Call line to claim our tickets, I realized I had left my ID in the room.

With three people in front of me, Matt strapped on his backpack, turned to me, and said, "Time me."

Off he sprinted, like an adult male version of Dora the Explorer, all the way to the hotel room. Right as I was called to the window, Matt came bounding back through the crowds—just in time.

So initially, the adventure of hiking all over the rainforest appealed to him. But as he soon found out, even Matt Dodd has limits.

Matt, Zach, and Joey (who flew in for the occasion) completed the first survey on foot due to the steep cost of hiring a helicopter.

What was supposed to be a five-day hike through the jungle quickly deteriorated into a nine-day trek filled with sickness, almost no communication, and shoes held together by nothing but literal strings by the end.

Downtown Disney it was not.

Still, the trip was successful as the men were able to survey a handful of villages, using a stick in the ground to communicate each point they would want to do if we moved in: language learning, literacy, Bible translation, and preaching the gospel.

One night, they entered a village to survey, and Matt became sick, hardly able to interact with the people at all.

The name of the village was Mawerero.

Little did he know that the mountain ridge in which he spent the night fevering would be the same one where he would begin building his house just months later.

When the men returned from that first survey, there was not much clarity about where to go.

Matt prayed:

3/29/2015
"God, it's Monday morning, and I'm sitting in our living room in Madang. We just got back from our first survey hike yesterday, and I'm tired and slightly feeling like I have a cold.

"God, oh, please help us. Please help us to make a decision, to think through all this information. God, I know You are sovereign over all things, and that You love us. Who shall separate us from the love of Christ?

"Jesus, You love me. You died for me. There is nothing in this world that changes that love. This last week of hiking through the bush did not change that love.

"O God, please help us to get along as a team as well. God, I pray that we can plan the next set of surveys and be able to find a place that needs to hear the gospel…just like I needed to hear the gospel, and then be able to preach to this place the good news of Jesus Christ!"

After another survey, this time in a helicopter with Jeremy Lehman, the men narrowed the list down to just two villages.

The final step was for the wives to visit and give feedback.

Again, the helicopter was scheduled and again, Mawerero made the list of villages to visit.

SING SINGS AND RICE

We were treated to a *sing sing* in both villages.

A *sing sing* is a performance involving traditional dress, dance, and songs in the people's Tok Ples—their language.

Staying in the village was a crazy experience, even coming from Madang. Sleeping in a hut with nothing but the bamboo floor, with rodents and insects scurrying up the walls, and a fire pit in the center was, if not comfortable, certainly unique.

There were no windows or holes in the roof to allow the smoke to escape (too much rain). But ventilation concerns aside, somehow being in a hut with a small fire going, the pitter-patter of rain falling on the roof, our teammates next to us, talking to the people of the village felt cozy.

The generosity of both villages to perfect strangers was extravagant. In addition to the *sing sings*, both villages offered ground upon which we could build our houses—even it meant them felling many trees to clear it for us. Both killed a chicken to feed us (meat is scarce up in those mountains) and served us a meal of bitter greens, chicken, and rice.

At the end of the trip, both had invited us to move in.

When we came home, it was with mixed feelings.

How could we pick between the two, when both desperately needed the gospel?

And yet, God is sovereign, and we could only go to one.

We discussed, we debated, we prayed, and, finally, we made a decision.

Our new home would be the village of Mawerero.

Housebuilding began in September of 2015 when a team flew from the US to help us build the two houses in the village.

Originally, we thought we could build both houses in two weeks with this team.

But, as we were learning, the only thing predictable about Papua New Guinea was its unpredictability.

When the plane landed with our friends from back home, we were overjoyed. My mom was on that plane with them, true to her pattern of visiting us wherever we were in the world.

The team's trip fell during Matt's birthday, and on that day, he wrote this:

9/13/2015

"God, thank You for making me. It's been a good 35 years. Here I sit in PNG and lots of our friends are here from the US. God, thank You for this time we have had with them. Thank You for saving me.

"God, I know I'm not like missionaries that have come before me, to the degree of godliness. Please, though, God, please make us godly men and women. I pray that we would be diligent to fight our sin and to know You more. Please encourage my own heart in all of this to remember why we are here. Please God, may we finish these houses!!

"God, it all makes me miss home. It makes me miss the people at home. And yet, God, what a good reminder that this world is not our home."

While it felt good to know where we were going, the decision was agonizing. Because, by saying yes to one, we were saying "no" to the other.

While God is sovereign over every unreached language, the need for someone to go is very real. To this day, the village we said 'no' to has not had the gospel go to it.

HOLDING HANDS WITH AN ANGRY, DRUNK MAN

Turns out we underestimated the challenges that came with building two houses in a helicopter-access-only village.

Due to its remote location, all the building supplies first had to be loaded onto a boat for a three-hour journey to the beach nearest our village.

Then, because the water was not deep enough for the boat to make it to shore, the supplies had to be transferred into dinghies. From the shore, each piece of lumber and box of screws had to be carried by hand several hundred feet away to the landing field where the helicopter could then pick them up and fly them into the village—one load at a time.

And that all had to happen before one nail could be hammered or one solar panel could be installed.

Through much perseverance and back-breaking labor, the lumber, screws, and other supplies had nearly all made it into the village—when Matt suddenly got a crash course in cultural awareness.

As the helicopter was on its last few loads, only Matt and a few other guys remained at the beach to load the remaining supplies, along with a few people from Mawerero who had hiked down to help.

We had just finished paying the dinghy guys who had helped us transfer our supplies from the boat to the beach.

Or so we thought.

See, in our American thinking, we paid the main guy we had been dealing with and instructed him to pay the other individuals who had helped.

Which he promptly did not.

Upon receiving no pay for his work, one of the dinghy drivers, drunk and angry, walked up to one of our new friends from Mawerero and punched him in the face.

Immediately, the beach erupted into a brawl.

Having no idea what had set the man off, Matt quickly and calmly went up to the angry man, took him by the hand, and began walking with him away from the commotion.

In Papua New Guinea culture, it's common for friends—both men and women—to hold hands during an entire conversation.

Matt walked with this angry gentleman, holding his hand and listening to him, for over an hour.

Eventually, he understood what had happened and we were able to make restitution. Matt joined the team with the rest of the supplies the next day, having learned a lesson in PNG culture, as well as the value of being a peacemaker.

The first team wasn't able to build both houses during their trip. But they were able to build one.

And eventually, after three more building trips, five months, and much perseverance, the houses were far enough along for both families to move in.

With only thick, black plastic wrapped around the frame of our houses separating us from the elements, the Dodds and Canns officially moved into the village of Mawerero on February 26, 2016.

Where Are All the Birds?

Mawerero was awe-inspiringly beautiful.

Built on a mountain ridge jutting out over the valley below and below the mountains above, it was home to several hundred people in the surrounding area.

From our front porch, the panoramic picture was all jungle and sky and mountains and waterfalls.

There was a whole bevy of new sights and sounds to get used to.

Young children scaling forty-foot-high palm trees to procure betelnut for their parents, chickens pecking at the smorgasbord that was the jungle ground, pigs roaming free and snuffling any scraps they could find.

At night, the dark shapes of bats were outlined against the brilliantly starry night sky and, in the background of it all, were the deafening notes of the insect symphony.

Curiously, while we would see birds flying in the valley below us or far above us, we rarely saw them fly through the village. And we would wonder, where are all the birds?

We soon figured it out.

One day as I was walking through the village, I saw a bird flying fairly close above us.

Just as I was marveling that finally, there was a bird, a commotion erupted around me. Suddenly, every man within firing distance quickly whipped out a slingshot and began shooting.

The bird escaped—barely.

The bird learned something that day and so did I.

Meat was scarce in the village and a bird is just as good a meal as any.

KIDS, COUNT THE WATERFALLS!

Living off of solar panels and a large water tank, the weather dictated much of our life in the village.

We had sun most mornings and would hurry as soon as it was up to throw our clothes into our solar-powered washing machine and hang them to dry on the line outside. It was a daily race between drying our clothes and the rain.

The urgency was real, as every afternoon around noon, thick swaths of clouds would descend on our village, enveloping it in mist and fog.

The clouds were so thick at times we could no longer see the mountains around us. Every day, they literally rolled straight through our house.

Were the clothes in our drawers damp most of the time? Sure.

Did I have a weekly routine of cleaning mold off my walls with bleach? Of course.

But was it the most amazing display of natural beauty that we got to witness nearly every day? Absolutely.

And on the rare, clear nights, all the stars would come out, brighter than someone from a city like Phoenix can imagine, and just hang there, clear and twinkling, better than any planetarium show.

And there were other natural wonders to behold.

Every week or so, an earthquake would shake the stilts on which our house was built—and those of every hut in our village.

At night, sometimes we would hear a landslide, the roar of breaking, rolling rocks and wake up in the morning to see a bare strip of land on the opposite hillside where a garden used to be.

And then there was the rain.

In the rainy season—one of the two seasons in Papua New Guinea, the other being *dry*, it would sometimes rain for days. Our roofs were made of corrugated metal so when it poured, we had to shout to hear each other over the beautiful, thunderous sound.

The big waterfall, which ran most of the year and was the village's primary water source, would turn into this monstrous, muddy mess, pouring down the mountainside like an overflowing pitcher of gurgling, magnificent brown water.

After the rain, I would walk out onto our porch with my kids and say, "Kids, count the waterfalls!" Wherever we looked, waterfalls streamed out of the mountains all around us. They never lasted for very long, but it was majestic while they did.

There were other elements about living in the village that I wasn't as enthusiastic about.

Like the insects. Some were super cool-looking—like the ones that lived *outside* the house. Others were not—like the ones that tried to live on your pillow. But, bugs were a small price to pay for us to have finally made it into the village!

OUR ACCIDENTAL PET

2/28/2016

"God, it's Sunday morning and we are in Mawerero! God, still crazy that we are here! Thank You that I can sit here, look out the window at a waterfall, hear the waterfall, and we can be with the people, and eat and take showers, and drink, and we don't have to move junk anymore! Oh God, I can't believe that we are here! Thank You, God. Now God, once again, You have put us in a situation where we need to depend on You.

"Please God, help us to live godly lives, to be diligent here, to be wise as serpents and innocent as doves. Please may our food and propane supplies last. Please give us wisdom on how to fix everything that is broken. Please provide the wisdom that we need to navigate these waters and please, God, make us godly people, make us worthy of bringing the gospel message to the people of Papua New Guinea!"

By far, the best part about that mountain ridge was the people.

While trying to integrate into a new language and culture is intimidating and uncomfortable at best, the people were always ready with smiles and conversation in Tok Pisin. We quickly learned that the best time to talk to people was when they were outside—like at market on Saturday mornings where you might find such treasures as bananas, sweet potatoes, taro, greens, and the occasional gem of a red onion or avocado. Or, when they were working in their gardens built into the impossibly steep mountainsides.

Matt was just as gregarious and engaging in a remote mountain village in Papua New Guinea as he was in Arizona or Santa Cruz or East Asia.

He knew that while people might not understand his words right away, everyone understood a smile.

And Matt smiled a lot.

As no one in the village understood English, he was constantly trying to make jokes in Tok Pisin—with varying degrees of success.

People laughed a lot more *at* Matt than they did *with* him at first, and Matt was just fine with that.

He was constantly out with the people, shaking hands, playing soccer with the kids. He was still ridiculous with animals, pretending to eat live lizards or putting a cat in his pocket.

The people loved him.

He was also totally unafraid to make mistakes in language learning.

One day, Matt and I were talking with some village ladies about my mom, who was making her second trip out to visit us in the village.

He had always been close with my mom and was excitedly talking about her arrival when in one of his sentences, he said my mom's name.

Quick as lightning, one of the older ladies reached out and slapped him.

Everyone who hailed from America was super confused in that moment.

Turns out, it's *tambu* for someone to mention the name of their mother-in-law: forbidden.

That was the day that Matt learned that a little temperance in language learning is a good thing.

We were all babies in language, pointing at things and asking what they were in Tok Pisin. But the people were patient with us, even appointing each of us a language helper, and bit by bit, we began to make progress, even if that progress was just beginning to know things by name.

But there are dangers of miscommunication when you are learning a language.

Such as when your eight-year-old tries her best to say in Tok Pisin, "I like your cat", but accidentally says, "I'd like your cat" instead, on the first day we arrived in the village.

That's how you end up with a mangy, undersized, lice-infested black cat that are now obligated to keep and raise as your own.

Matt and the kids were thrilled.

I was not.

Missing our homeland, we named the cat Hawaii.

HAWAII, THE LICE-INFESTED CAT

Turned out, all Hawaii needed was a little food.

Before long, the cat became sleek and fat. Always on the small side, he fit right in with being a Dodd.

From day one, Matt loved Hawaii, lice and all. He continued his long-standing tradition of being ridiculous with animals, stuffing Hawaii under his shirt with just the poor cat's face poking out at the top or putting him in drawers or on shelves or some other place he didn't belong. Not even lice could deter this part of Matt.

Hawaii was more than a pet; he was useful.

Along with the insects, rats were our ever-present houseguests in those first few months. Every night, we would set out a trap and, in the morning, like clockwork, there would be a new rat in the cage.

Enter Hawaii's special skill set.

All we had to do was open the cage, and, in seconds, the rat was gone. Only the tail and bones came back up.

Slightly disturbing to watch, but useful.

The first few months of life in the village were pretty stressful as we attempted to balance language learning, homeschooling, and time with the people.

Big financial and cultural decisions had to be made every day, and being unanimous with our co-workers was still a struggle.

But there were millions of bright spots.

One was the secret passageway Matt built between our kids' rooms. It was just a slab of wood that could be pulled up or down, but sneaking into the girls' room to steal their Legos or vice versa became a favorite pastime of our ten, nine, six, and four-year-olds.

Matt found new ways to exercise—everything from doing pull-ups on the exposed beams of our ceilings to yoga in the living room to hiking all around the village with Mary on his back like a cute, blond, curly-haired monkey.

Still eager to take on physical challenges, Matt agreed to another one when my cousin, Josh, flew out for a visit. Helicopter flights aren't cheap and Josh, being the savvy, thrifty guy that he is, decided that he would pay for the heli flight in, but not out. Instead, he opted for the ten-hour hike out of the village to the beach, followed by a three-hour dinghy ride to town the next morning.

Matt, wearing the genuine smile of hospitality, volunteered to accompany him down, see him off in the morning, and then hike back. This he did, but by the time they reached the beach, Matt got a fever. Fevering most of the night, he saw Josh off the next morning, and then proceeded to hike the ten hours all the way back up to the village—in the now-pouring rain. When he finally made it home, he was sick and exhausted.

Even our village friend who accompanied them on the trip told Matt that he wouldn't be doing that again anytime soon.

A Bad Case of Strep

Meanwhile, the work we came to do proved to be difficult.

Learning a new language, one that isn't written down and where no resources are available to aid you, is challenging. Even with language helpers, our progress was slow and tedious. We had to be willing, among other things, to be laughed at quite a bit by the people as we feebly tried to repeat their words and phrases.

And then there was the culture.

Trying to navigate a culture where when one gives a cabbage, there is an unspoken expectation of something of equivalent value in return, has its own obstacles.

What is the equivalent of a cabbage? Is it an empty plastic Coke bottle they can use as a future canteen? Is it an old T-shirt? Value systems in our village were very different than ours, and learning them was no easy feat.

On top of those things, there was just the daily life of a family of six.

Making food from scratch, measuring our natural resources (in the rainy season, we had plenty of water, but had to ration our solar power; during the dry season it was the other way around, etc.), meticulously calculating the weight of our supplies for the helicopter on our next supply run (in the metric system again!), while still trying to teach kindergarten through fifth grade made each day full and often chaotic.

It was easy on some days to feel as though we were doing none of it well.

In July, Matt and I decided to take our first break out of the country in two years and go to Australia.

As we were making these plans, our oldest daughter, Susanna came down with strep throat. We gave her antibiotics and watched it go away.

But a few weeks later, right before our break, the strep came back. Again we treated her with antibiotics, watched the fevers go down, and she was fine.

Off we went to Australia, checking off things from our Australian bucket list such as seeing huge, salt-water crocodiles, cuddly, sleepy koalas, and slightly-miffed-looking kangaroos. The kangaroos' demeanor was understandable as they were in a pen where people could walk around and pet them, and Matt was, once again, trying to get closer to an animal's face than normal.

We boarded the plane back to Papua New Guinea, refreshed and ready to come back to the village, when Susanna spiked a fever *again*.

It was strep for the third time and took longer to resolve this time with higher fevers and worse symptoms, but eventually it went away.

We began consulting with some friends from the medical community back home. A tonsillectomy was brought up as a possibility, but we hoped that wouldn't be necessary.

But two weeks later, when she got it again, we had to start seriously considering it.

Not only was it becoming more and more likely that Susanna was a chronic carrier of strep, each time it came back, her symptoms had worsened.

Higher fevers.

Tonsils so swollen she could not swallow water.

We lived in a helicopter-access-only location. The possibility of a seizure or something worse was real, and we had to weigh that.

A return home to the US was not at all what we were planning on. As far as we could see, this would only be a huge interruption of everything we were in the middle of.

Susanna was sick more and more of the time, and we let Hawaii sleep in bed with her, lice and all, since he was the only one who brought her joy in those moments. This led to Matt giving him the moniker: 'Hawaii the Comfort Kitty."

When the strep came back again only a week after the bout before, we had an extremely difficult decision to make.

Did we leave and take Susanna to the US to get a tonsillectomy and make it an early furlough?

Did we try to wait it out to see if maybe it wouldn't come back?

We sought counsel from our pastors, from an ENT, from nurses back home, and we prayed.

An extremely kind and generous couple in the States sent us money that would cover the whole cost of our family coming home, just so we didn't have to think about the finances.

We had just decided to send Susanna and myself back to mitigate the interruption in language learning, when Onesimus, our six-year-old—woke up with his second occurrence of strep throat in six weeks.

The ENT back home thought it was a possibility that both kids might be carriers of the bacteria and might both potentially need tonsillectomies.

We made the decision to go back as a family.

We looked our new village friends in the eye and said, "We'll see you in six months!"

We waved to Cass and Zach and to Jeremy and Lorie, our very dear co-workers, and said the same: "See you in six months!"

God knew that that would not be the case.

He knew that day, that that would be the last time Matt would see any of those sweet faces on this earth.

We had one plan for our family, but He had another, better plan.

And quietly, He was working it out.

GREETING THE LAST NEW YEAR

In September of 2016, we boarded a plane—the first of many—and made the long trip back to America.

Shortly after we got back, Susanna got strep throat again, and we treated it only to watch it come back a week later…again. This was so kind of God as it served as confirmation that we had made the right decision to come back.

In October, the tonsillectomy was performed, and in one more of God's gracious and totally undeserved provisions for our family, he had the anesthesiologist, the surgeon, the nurses, and the surgical center volunteer to do it free of charge.

This was beyond anything we could have asked for or hoped, and it was right around that time that I stopped being surprised by anything that God might do for us.

But something else began happening in October.

Matt began having some strange symptoms that we couldn't quite figure out.

Numbness on the left side of his body occasionally.

Strange sensations in his left hand.

And then came the bizarre incident on our family outing where he could not control the flashes of dreams in his vision for six hours.

We met with a neurologist who was not concerned about Matt's symptoms or even his six-hour episode. Matt had had migraines since college, and the neurologist was convinced that they were just side effects from those.

But an MRI was scheduled just in case.

We celebrated Thanksgiving, and we celebrated Christmas.

We decided to cast our cares on the Lord, hope all things, and not be anxious.

To this day, I do not regret one day of that waiting where I chose not to be anxious.

Matt's symptoms continued and grew slightly more frequent, but we put stock in the neurologist's words and called it migraine side effects.

We did not know, of course, that those would be our last holidays spent as a family.

We did not know that those would be the last weeks where we would be thinking and planning hard about how our lives should look once we got back to Papua New Guinea.

We did not know a lot of things.

But God knew.

God knew, and He loved us, and He had brought us back to the United States *because* He knew and because He loved us.

He had one perfect plan for our family and for Matt Dodd.

For years, God had been teaching Matt about His faithfulness in trials, and Matt had seen that rope of God's faithfulness hold fast time and again.

One more time, Matt's faith would be tried, tested, and proved as we unknowingly greeted the new year that would bring Matt finally home.

Matt taking a selfie with Pais, one of the men from our village, and an unsuspecting lizard.

Aerial photo of our village of Mawerero.

Matt (left) and Zach (with baby Oliver) at a sing-sing.

Family picture in Mawerero.

Hawaii, the comfort kitty.

Matt returning home and hugging the kids.

UNSHAKEABLE JOY

Part II

A Change in Direction

JANUARY

CHAPTER 7

Held Fast

January 10, 2017 *(Facebook Update)*

In a sovereignly ordained change of events for our lives, we found ourselves in the ER last night. It started with an MRI for Matt where several lesions were found in his brain and where they told us to go straight to the ER. We are currently at Barrow Neurological Institute where they're running tests to determine if these growths are cancerous tumors or perhaps an infection. There's a surgery tentatively scheduled for Thursday depending on how the tests come back.

Either way, our lives took an unexpected turn yesterday and it has been a strange and challenging 24 hours. We are so thankful for MRIs and Barrow and doctors. We're thankful to be in this country where we can get whatever is going on diagnosed. And we're thankful to be surrounded by people who love us and care for us as we try to get this figured out.

While there is much we don't know, what we do know is crucial: God is sovereign--He is completely in control of Matt's body and cells; He is good--He loves us and gave His Son that we might have our sins forgiven and have the hope to spend eternity with Him; and He is faithful. We have been privileged to see His faithfulness for the last two years in PNG and know He will not abandon us now.

We are looking to Him and waiting on Him to direct our steps! Were there something better for us than those MRI results or this hospital room, He would have given that to us instead. But He didn't, and we trust that His ways are not our ways--they're better.

Please pray that this would just be an infection as that sounds like it might be the best-case scenario. Pray that if it's His will, God would

heal Matt. And pray that regardless of test results or outcome, we would love the Lord more than our lives or each other and that He would be glorified in this!

At the time, we had no idea that 'lesion' is synonymous with 'tumor'.

We knew nothing about cancer or any of the other terms we suddenly began hearing. All that we really knew was that whatever was going on inside Matt's body wasn't good.

Sitting in that emergency room, there was a lot going on around us that was frightening.

With the ER filled to capacity, we were stationed on a bed in the hall where there were quite a few nurses running around and patients moaning and yelling.

Matt, who had never liked being around blood, was suddenly seeing quite a bit of it. Nurse after nurse tried to get an IV in him, but all failed, leaving needles and blood on the bedside.

With every failed attempt, Matt would just smile and thank the most recent nurse for trying.

All of this was frightening.

But though we were scared of the situation, we were not scared of the outcome.

Matt was smiling and still making jokes, not because the situation was not serious, but because he knew Who was in control of it and trusted Him.

When I first got to his side, before I could open my mouth, he was already reminding me of what was still true. And with each new family member or friend who rotated in and out of the hospital that night, he did the same.

This had blindsided us, he was quick to say, but God was not surprised by it.

God was still sovereign over these circumstances and in fact, intended them for our good! He who did not spare His own Son, but gave Him up for us all, how will He not also with Him graciously give us all things? (Rom. 8:32)

Certainly, we could trust the One who had provided for our greatest need to provide for us in this smaller one. Our circumstances did not change the character of God—Psalm 119:68 was just as true on this day as it had been the day before, "You are good and do good." Matt declared to all in that emergency room that his biggest problem was not cancer or death; it was his sin and that problem had been solved long ago by Jesus on the cross.

To every anxious face that came to visit him, Matt was quick to assure them that this was the Lord's will for his life and that He was still good.

But still, he really did not like needles.

Eventually, we made it into a room upstairs, and, with the help of an ultrasound, the nurses finally got a line in Matt.

The next two days were filled with CT scans, more MRIs, a steady stream of rotating doctors…and information.

Lots of information.

Nothing would be conclusive until the biopsy three days later, but every hour brought new pieces of the puzzle that God already had put together before the foundation of the world.

Sometimes, those pieces threatened to break our hearts.

But God's grace was sufficient to hold us together.

As we braced ourselves in that calm before the storm, Matt's journal entry from the night he was admitted illustrates just how well he was upheld by that grace:

> *"God, it's Tuesday night, and I'm sitting in a hospital bed! God, what seemingly strange plans You have for us sometimes. No one, though, ever sees cancer, sickness, or days in the hospital as ever a good idea. Yet, God, I don't know, this is Your perfect plan for us. God, really I just didn't see this one coming!! God, please may this be an infection. I think that would be better.*
>
> *"But how do I know what is better? Perhaps this is exactly what You want for us…cancer or something like that? Thank You, God, for Your many mercies in all of this…financial support, a good room, great doctors. I just don't know if You brought us back here just so I could die. It seems like You have something*

more in store for us. God, please may we be able to do this. Please provide the grace that we need to do this!"

Over the years, we had been through some trials—a permanent disability, a miscarriage—but never had something so shaken our world as to make us completely lose our grip on the mountain we were climbing together.

This was *that* phone call. *That* report from the doctor. *That* event that changes everything.

Suddenly, there was nothing left to hold on to.

Our hands gave out, and, in a split second, we were falling to the rocks below, just like me off that cliff.

Except we didn't.

Because at the exact moment when we had no strength left to hold onto the rope, that unbreakable, unfailing rope held onto us.

The One who held it knew the measure of our strength and when it would run out, and on that day, He was faithful to lend us His.

January 11, 2017 *(Facebook Update)*

With each new day, more information comes in about what might be going on with Matt. This morning, we learned that Matt's CT scan yesterday revealed nodules all over his body. It seems that whatever is going on, it is everywhere. The three options on the table at this point are infectious disease, strange tumors, or lymphoma.

The plan right now is to perform a biopsy on one of the growths in Matt's brain tomorrow and do some pathology on it to see what kind of tissue it is. From there, we'll know more about next steps.

Throughout all of this, we are reminded again and again about who God is. In His good and perfect plan and timing, here we sit. But He who has ordained this for us is also our rock, our shield, and our refuge. Never have the words of the Psalms or Scripture in general felt quite so real and applicable. We are thankful that He has given us this trial so that we can know Him better and fasten our gaze on Him in a way we haven't had to before.

Our hope ultimately is not in any diagnosis--brain tumor, cancer, disease. God already knows what it is. What matters is where we look with a diagnosis and without and where we run with good news and with bad. God is so good to us, to be with us every step of this way.

Please pray that the surgery tomorrow would be helpful in finding a diagnosis; pray that whatever it might be, that there might be treatment; and pray that above all, our eyes and our hearts would be set on Him who made us and saved us and knows us and loves us far more than any doctor could or more than we could love each other.

Matt, being the forever optimist that he was, hoped that this might all prove to be some strange infectious disease he had contracted in Papua New Guinea.

This was looking less and less likely as the tumors in his brain were more indicative of cancer, but he held out hope.

I don't remember exactly when it was that I first saw Matt's MRI, but I remember being horrified. There were not only a dozen tumors on his brain, there were shadows where past bleeds had occurred, with the biggest one on his right frontal lobe. Hence, all the strange symptoms happening on the left side of his body.

Ultimately, when all the scans were done and all the doctors had had their say, we decided we needed a biopsy to be sure.

Matt had been working for weeks on a sermon he planned to preach at one of our supporting churches in California the following week.

Here is what Matt wrote to that pastor:

"Gary,

Just to give you a quick update. The CT scan I had the other day revealed several abnormalities like lymph nodes in my abdomen that are swollen, growths on some of my bones, nodules in my lungs, and I think a few other things. All these are still indicative of either an infectious disease or cancer…So yes, I'm asking you to pray or keep praying that there are microbes or an infection in my brain! :)

We are trusting the Lord in all of this, and there is much to be thankful for. We're thankful for good doctors, a nice room, the love of church family, many *prayers, and impromptu dates we are taking too! (Yes, the dates are all at the hospital but still…), how God brought us back to the US apparently to take care of this as well!*

This morning when one doctor described the neurological surgeon and what good hands I'll be in and how smart he is, I just thought, yes, I AM in good hands. I am in the hands of a loving Father, who is infinitely wise, and cares for me. He cares for us and He is in control of all this. He is the great physician. He heals the sick, opens blind eyes, and raises the dead! And He has already taken away my biggest problem — the wrath I deserve!

I'm still preparing to preach, however there are a few scenarios that could happen that would obviously change that…

In His Hands,
Matt Dodd

"'For I consider that the sufferings of this present time are not worth comparing with the glory that is to be revealed to us'" (Romans 8:18, ESV).

Matt's primary goal going into his biopsy was courage to honor Christ, by life or by death, and to continue striving to be that *kind* of man—in sickness and health.

The morning of his biopsy, Matt wrote in his journal:

"God, it's Thursday morning, and I'm still in the ICU. I get surgery today. God, please help me today. I have no idea what this day is going to hold; what tomorrow holds. So far You have been gracious, and though at times hard, it's been good. Everything may change.

"God, please sustain us. Help me be content with pain and discomfort. Please help Cameron to be able to handle whatever news comes, and please may I not at all be ashamed, but that with full courage now as always Christ will be honored in my body, whether by life or by death.

"God, please give me joy and contentment today. My joy is not in my circumstances, or how I feel, or the diagnosis, but my joy is in You! God, please help me. Please be with Cameron today as well. In all of this, God, may I still love my wife, and love my kids, and still care for my family well, even when I don't feel good.

"I do pray that this would be something simple, God—something that can be taken care of easily. God, whatever Your will is, please use these circumstances to fight our sin, become more holy, love You more, hope in heaven, and trust You. Please God, may we not be shaken by this!"

In our hearts and to each other, Matt and I kept reminding one another, "(The righteous man) is not afraid of bad news; his heart is firm, trusting in the LORD" (Psalm 112:6-7).

Bad news would indeed come this day, but, by God's grace alone, we were not afraid.

CHAPTER 8

"That's the Lord's Will"

January 12, 2017 *(Facebook Update)*

In God's good plan, we learned today that what we've been seeing on Matt's scans is cancer.

The doctors have sent the tissue out for pathology to find out what kind it is--where it originated in his body. Because what the doctor found when he operated today was a tumor, it's likely that the nodules they've been finding elsewhere in Matt's body are also tumors.

So.

It was not good news.

No one, I think, would ever choose cancer or sickness. But it was also the best news in that God told us today that the best thing for Matt, for myself, and for our kids is cancer.

We are not sure of so many things ahead. There will undoubtedly be hard days to come. But all I can say is that today was a good day because the Lord made it and we can rejoice and be glad in Him. He has given us so much good and should we who are but clay speak when He gives us something like this? We are sinners and He has reconciled us to Himself at the cost of His own Son. His love for us is sure.

God has given me so much peace and contentment today—as I write this right now, but also when I was given the news by the doctor when Matt was still not awake. And God gave me many helps along the way. He gave me a kind and competent doctor who probably has to give bad news a lot and does it well, as well as friends and family to be with me at the time so I was not alone.

My biggest concern perhaps was having to tell Matt--which I ended up having to do, like, 10 times as he was coming out of the anesthesia (really not what I wanted to keep repeating in different ways and in different tones of voice, but that, too, was God's plan) and seeing his reaction. But Matt's reaction was to point out that in the past when he had seen other people get cancer, he thought God must have thought their faith strong enough to handle it and then he said, "I guess it's kind of an honor to get cancer. I mean, not everybody gets cancer."

So, we are well in the Lord. He is our refuge and our strength. We love Him and trust that the plan He's working out is the very best one. Naked we came into this world and naked we'll leave; blessed be the name of the Lord who loves us and does not leave us when we need Him most.

Please pray that we would trust God with whatever the diagnosis ends up being. God already knows. Pray that it would be treatable, that Matt would be healed if that would be God's will. Pray for our family members and our teammates in PNG whom this news impacts most directly. Pray that we would just keep our eyes fixed on Him and not horses or chariots or disease.

I waited in the Bret Michaels Hospitality and Music room with my family and one of our pastors, Smedly Yates, during the biopsy.

As we sat together in this pleasant room with its plush new furniture and colorful guitars on the wall, conversation was kept mostly light-hearted as the surgery minutes ticked by.

We asked the question, who was Bret Michaels and why was his face on the walls of this room. Someone else spent a seriously disproportionate amount of time making a rousing defense about why Jaws was one of the best movies ever made. Every person knew why we were there. We knew what we were waiting for.

And yet, the weight of the waiting seemed lighter with others along to help me carry it. I was so thankful to not be alone.

God was kind to guard my heart from being anxious during that time—a supernatural response for me since my heart is prone to anxiety. There was literally a season in our marriage where I was honest-to-goodness, having-chest-pains anxious that I was going to die by killer whale.

Not the most rational fear, especially considering the fact that we lived in Phoenix. It had started in 2010, when an orca killed a trainer at Sea World. I had read article after article about similar incidents and, somehow, this culminated in me being pretty certain that I, too, would meet my end in the maw of an orca.

Eventually, God helped me see this irrational anxiety as sin. All that to say, it went against my nature not to be anxious.

But God gave me grace to not be anxious that day about things which I did not yet know for sure and to trust that when I did, He would help me then, too.

When Dr. Francisco Ponce, our neurosurgeon, entered, I stood to greet him and breathed a prayer for grace to hear whatever news God would have me hear.

It was not a brain infection.

It was not lymphoma.

It was Stage IV metastasized cancer; originating somewhere else in the body and spreading to everywhere else, including the brain.

I nodded. I thanked him—this man who must have to deliver such news to people every day.

And slowly, as he talked, I began to grasp that this was very, very bad news.

He left, and I sat down with this group of now silent people who had heard that definitive gavel slam the same as I had.

Excusing myself, I made my way to Matt's empty ICU room and wept.

I wasn't confused, and I wasn't angry; I was just very sad.

There was something terrible in the fact that I not only knew this news before Matt, but that I would have to be the one to tell him.

As I was guided to the post-op room where Matt was waking up, I prayed for courage.

If there was going to be a tipping point in how we were going to walk through this ordeal, I knew that it would be right here, in how Matt responded to this news.

As Matt slowly came out of anesthesia, he asked me what the result of the biopsy was.

"It's cancer," I said with an ache in my voice and waited to see how my best friend would respond.

Would he weep and lament God's plan?

Demand an audience with God or ask why like Job?

Beg God for more time like Hezekiah?

And now, here is the sweet part of having the wretched job of messenger.

I got to witness first-hand how my husband responded to such devastating news.

"Bummer," he said. And then he said something to the effect of, "Well, that's the Lord's will. I mean, I guess it's kind of an honor. Not everybody gets cancer."

And then he promptly forgot the whole conversation as the anesthesia was still flushing itself out of his system. He asked me again what the doctor had said.

I had to tell him the same horrible news about six or seven more times.

And do you know?

That man responded the same way.

Every. Single. Time.

God had been cultivating humility in Matt for a very long time that expressed itself in submitting to His plan for his life without delay.

A common saying around our house in the years leading up to this moment whenever things would go wrong—big things, inconvenient things, small things—was "That's the Lord's will." The idea being that God has one good plan and that this bad thing, whatever it might be, is part of it. So, we can still rejoice even though it is not what we would have chosen because God chose it for us and is working it for our good because He is good!

Ultimately, the distance between Matt learning of God's decreed will for his life, and wholly submitting himself—indeed, volunteering himself for that decreed will—was seconds, not minutes or days or weeks.

Matt's response upon waking up from his biopsy was what I expected him to say, although I wasn't sure he would until he said it. To hear him say it, the same thing he had been saying for years, in light of this news proved yet again the indefatigability of God's truth and promises.

By God's grace, Matt had built his house upon the rock of God's character and His promises. His was a foundation built of eternal, all-powerful, unchanging truth, and so when the waves of temporal circumstances raged, when the floods came, and the rain fell, and the winds blew and beat against it, it did not fall.

This was Matt's testimony on that first day of bad news, and, by God's grace, it would be so until his last.

January 14, 2017 *(Facebook Update)*

Late in the afternoon yesterday, we received a preliminary diagnosis: Stage 4 lung cancer.

This information seems stark to us because we now have a name to call what is going on other than just the general umbrella of 'cancer'. And yet, we are simply learning about something God has known about since before we were born. We process this information with tears over the very real practical difficulties that lie ahead, assuming this is the diagnosis. We also process it with praise--because God only gives good gifts to His children.

God chose this road for us long ago--it is now just a matter of us finding out about it and walking it. Now, we, too, get to choose this road. We, too, get to humble ourselves under the hand of God that is just as abundant in power as it is in goodness and wisdom. We get to say yes to something that God decided before the foundations of the earth would bring Him glory and us good.

I can't help thinking also that this is still not what we deserve. I would ask why bad things happen to good people if I thought there was anyone truly righteous before God.

Matt is a good man, but he is not righteous before God and neither am I. We're both sinners, deserving an eternity in hell to repay the debt we owe God. But God set his love on us when we did not love Him, and He rescued us from that sentence through Jesus His Son, who became our righteousness in life, our redeemer in death, and our absolute one-and-only Savior in His resurrection.

Therefore, when we hear lung cancer stage 4 and we compare it to an eternity spent away from the One who loves us best and is our best good, we smile.

Because cancer, though it wreaks havoc, destruction, and even death in our bodies, will never be able to touch our salvation, our inheritance, or our Savior who stands as our shield against this present flood of bad news and whose words make up the only rock upon which we stand.

This morning, when I woke up, I considered not really trying to get ready for the day. But then I remembered that we can't lose anything that matters most on this earth, that God is good, and that He will be just as faithful today as He was yesterday and has been this whole last week. So, I washed my salt-encrusted face and put on make-up that wouldn't hinder tears, and Matt and I walked out of the house together to tell our kids.

Please pray for us as this initial diagnosis has demanded we re-evaluate our future--immediate and long term. Pray that we can find housing as our living situation will need to change if chemotherapy is going to be a part of our lives. Pray for our insurance and finances as both will be complicated by this re-routing of our lives. Pray for our kids who have really been such troopers throughout the last several transitions and who we will need to ask to persevere through one more. Pray that the treatment for Matt would be effective, if that is the Lord's will. And pray that on the days where we can't smile, that God would uphold us for His ultimate glory and our ultimate good.

Stage IV lung cancer has frightening statistics.

Less than 4% of patients diagnosed at stage IV are alive five years later; 50% die within eight months. There are always outliers, but those are generally the numbers. We learned there is a lung cancer mutation that can happen in young non-smokers without much data as to why it occurs and it was into this category that Matt fell.

The more we learned about this diagnosis, the worse it seemed to get.

As we sat in that hospital, we knew that there were three practical things that would need to be addressed.

The first was our living situation.

We had been staying with a family from our church but had only been planning to be there temporarily until we returned to Papua New Guinea. With cancer and chemotherapy in the picture now, we knew we would need to find another place to live.

But where? And with what means?

The second thing was that we quite literally had nothing here.

No furniture, no personal items— everything we owned was back in our house in the village. We had come to the US on furlough with little more than the clothes on our backs.

How would we be able to start over?

The third issue was perhaps the hardest—our ministry in Papua New Guinea.

Would all that we had worked for and attempted to do be thwarted by this diagnosis?

It was such a small operation, made up of just a few families and a handful of supporting churches. Who cared about this small venture in the remote mountains of an island nation of which many people had never heard?

No place to live, no possessions, and an entire gospel work suddenly in jeopardy.

Three formidable obstacles about which, sitting in that hospital, we were relatively helpless to do anything.

But sometimes, I think, God has us encounter obstacles so staggering in their height and breadth just so that we can watch Him dwarf them in His power and goodness.

Witness Friday, the day after Matt's biopsy.

Before we had time to even fully identify these problems, while our heads were still spinning from the diagnosis, one of our pastors walked in.

"Someone from our church body would like to buy a house for you guys to live in," he said.

We were speechless.

Sure enough, after we were discharged from the hospital, we picked out a house the next Tuesday and it closed the following Wednesday.

If that had been the only instance of ridiculously generous love shown by our brothers and sisters in Christ during this time, it would have been enough for us to marvel at for the rest of our lives.

But it wasn't.

A few days later while I was driving, I received a phone call from another dear friend.

"Multiple people have contacted me who would like to buy furniture for your new house," she informed me. "As soon as you guys are able, you can go to a furniture store and pick out what you want."

I just shook my head.

Was there anything God couldn't do, if He wanted to?

He did indeed own the cattle on a thousand hills and to see the love of His people want to direct any of that to us was just very humbling.

But what about that small mountain work in Papua New Guinea?

God had His eye on that, too. Because He is the God of obscure island nations just the same as He is the God of the United States of America.

Although we did not see how, we knew even sitting in that hospital room that if God wanted the people of Mawerero to hear the gospel and be saved, there wasn't a force on earth that could stop it—not cancer or death or anything.

We didn't know it at the time, but God had already prepared another family on the other side of the world to take the baton from us.

Six months before Matt was diagnosed, one of our pastors had gone to South Africa and sent out a call for more laborers to go to the unreached peoples in PNG. A family by the name of the Mitchells had answered that call before he was even done preaching. If that were not enough—because God is able to do far more abundantly than all that we ask or imagine—there was a young, single lady at a different church in South Africa who also wanted to be a part of whatever team they were on.

So it was that on January 9th, while we were still reeling from a biopsy, a family on the other side of the world, whom we had never met, was already preparing to go to a village in PNG. As it turned out, that village would be ours.

Long before Matt was diagnosed, God had, in fact, raised up not just one family unit, but two, to take our place in the village of Mawerero. On the day he was diagnosed, they already had 60% of their support raised.

He had a plan all along so that the work of the gospel in our village would not stop.

Who cared about this small work in those remote mountains?

God cared!

He has one plan and, if needed, He'll bring people from South Africa to accomplish it!

We were discharged on a Saturday and sent home with an aggressive batch of steroids to help reduce the swelling caused by the tumors in Matt's brain. We took a moment at home together to mourn this unofficial diagnosis together. We did not know the above statistics yet, but we knew this was very bad news.

We were still sad.

But we were not hopeless.

Because when we knew nothing else, we knew that our hope—our treasure—was not in a new house or new furniture. It was not in a successful ministry in a remote village. It wasn't even in our kids or each other. It was in our Savior and in Him alone.

Before we had any of the answers to the above questions, Matt wrote this in his journal:

"God, I'm thankful for this time right now. I'm thankful that I can sit here and talk to you. I may not have much time here, but really won't I have all eternity to talk to You? Oh God, please give me strength to do this! Please God, for the sake of my family, and my friends, may I make it through this alive. I am truly thankful that You consider us worthy to suffer in this way.

"Please be glorified, God. Please take our anxieties away. God, it is a sad situation, but I mean I was never guaranteed a long life. I was never guaranteed an easy life. Really, what I deserve is not a long life. I deserve hell from a holy God; I deserve eternal separation from a loving God. That's what I deserve, but I'm not getting it. Truly, I am not getting what I deserve. There are some truths I've said before and half-meant. Now I really mean it, and I have to, because it is true!

"God, can You please help me with these things I am really worried about? I don't know how the finances are going to work. I don't know where we are going to live. Oh God, please help us. God, please comfort us in all of this. I am just really glad I know You, God. I'm glad I'm not in this alone and I never will be. That at least makes it all worth it. God, please help me to continue to love my wife, and my kids. Please may I be an exceptional father, an exceptional husband, even when I'm not feeling well. God, please may I be so diligent to seek You and to know You!"

Matt may not have been suffering because of persecution or martyrdom as he had once hoped, but his heart was to suffer in any way he could for the sake of the gospel, that Christ's name might be made known, and he pleaded for grace to do it well.

Our kids, at this point, did not know.

They knew there were possibilities of cancer and death on the table, but once cancer was confirmed to us, we knew we needed to tell them.

We picked up our kids from my parents' house, got on the freeway, and drove. We took some exit we didn't recognize on the way out of town and into the desert and pulled into the parking lot of a random industrial complex. No need to go to a familiar place and give our kids an unnecessary bad association with places they knew and loved.

From the front seat, Matt turned around and told our kids as gently and as straightforward as he could that Daddy had cancer.

In the back seat of our minivan, Susanna, ten years old at the time, immediately burst into tears.

What broke her heart in that moment was not first and most the diagnosis, as none of the kids were really able to understand what that meant then, but rather the fact that this news meant we would not be going back to PNG, where she had built a life and friends.

"Hey guys," Matt said, as he had said a thousand times before. "What do we say when things like this happen?"

"It's the Lord's will," all four of them quietly chorused.

"That's right," Matt agreed. "And we can trust Him."

Our pastors asked Matt if he would want to say a few things at church the following morning.

In the same way he had been striving not to waste his life, Matt was determined not to waste his cancer and immediately agreed. He wanted to use every opportunity he had to declare God's goodness.

Little did he know, this would be the last opportunity for a while where he would have all his faculties to do that.

CHAPTER 9

This Doesn't Change Your Goodness

January 15, 2017 (*Sunday - Matt Dodd addresses the body of Grace Bible Church in Tempe, AZ three days after his diagnosis.*):

First, I do want to say that we are doing well by God's grace! It's truly just been a week where we are grieving in this trial and yet rejoicing in the salvation of our God and just the love that we see.

A few years ago, there was a season of our marriage when Cameron and I were talking about ways we were afraid of dying.

Cameron brought up: "I'm afraid of dying 'death by Orca whale'. It is appropriate to laugh at that statement. I think it was technically 'plane crash into the ocean followed by death by Orca whale'.

To which my response as her husband was, "Listen, if you died 'death by Orca whale', that would clearly be the Lord's will for your life."

She's no longer in this place, but how could you argue with that, right? It's true! I mean, we're standing here, four months in the country from Papua New Guinea, and to hear the doctor say, "Stage IV lung cancer", how could we argue with this? This is clearly the Lord's will for our life.

When Job stood there, and servant after servant came and gave him bad news, he clearly knew that was the Lord's will for his life. And he responded with: "Naked I came into this world and naked I will return. The Lord gives and the Lord takes away."

This is God's will for our lives and we recognize that.

I wanted to share a couple of ways that we've seen the goodness of God in these circumstances. I am going to associate both of them with stories from Papua New Guinea, because who doesn't like hearing about Papua New Guinea, right?

First, one of the times we were trying to find a village into which we could move and preach the gospel, Zach and I were on one of the hardest hikes I had ever been on up to that point. We were hiking up to Yot Wam. We left at three in the morning from sea level. We hiked up to, like, 5,000 feet, then back down to 2,000 feet, and then we hiked back up to 4,000 feet. We got there at 6 pm. I just laid down on the floor as soon as we got there and slept till 6 am the next morning. I was so exhausted while we were hiking and around one in the afternoon, I thought, "I can't do this".

I sat down and put my head in my hands and I just thought, "Why am I doing this to myself? Why am I putting myself through all of this pain and suffering?" The next morning, I opened up the Bible, and reminded myself about the gospel, and I was like, "this is why".

It's worth it!

All the pain that I must suffer so these people we're meeting, that they might hear about Jesus Christ, that they just might repent and believe and know the one true God who is infinitely merciful--anything that it costs me, any pain that I must suffer, I mean, this is all just totally worth it.

Similarly, in this situation, as I lay in bed this past week, seemingly watching many things in my life pass away, I thought, "Is this the best plan?" And my response was, "Yes".

I can in confidence say this is the best plan. God is infinitely wise. He is infinitely good. Look, this isn't what we were thinking. I don't think anyone was thinking this. This is God's plan, and we are constantly being reminded just how undeserving we are of anything. We came into this world with nothing, we are leaving with nothing. We have already received grace upon grace in this life. Nobody promised 37 years of life. 36 is great!

And really our biggest problem is not cancer.

Our biggest problem by far is not cancer. My biggest problem is my sin. My biggest problem was that I was a slave of my sin. I was dead in my transgressions and sin. I was under the wrath of God, and God, in His grace and mercy at the cross of Jesus Christ, took my wrath so that I could be His son. So that He could adopt me and declare me righteous. That problem is gone! So, cancer is just small in comparison.

Secondly, we had some hard times in Papua New Guinea, you know, hard situations, hard circumstances. I remember with Zach, Jeremy, and I when we were going through various things, I would just pray, "God, please make this stop. This is just difficult." And yet, after they were all over, Zach, Jeremy and I would sit down, talk about those times, and we'd remember them with such fondness. Because there was such dependence!

Similarly, in this situation, I wake up in the morning and I'm praying prayers that I've never prayed before. You know, prayers like, "God, thank you for another day that I'm alive. God, please help me to make it through this day."

Just seeing the dependence on the Lord that God has created in this situation that He has sovereignly and wisely and goodly given us, is again just the kindness and goodness of God. Sometimes, I just think, "Why can't it always be like this? Why can't I just wake up every morning and be so thankful for another day and so dependent on the Lord to make it through this day?"

But man, sometimes we just need a trial to stir things up. We need a trial to help us love the Lord more. We need a trial to help us stir up love for one another and if I have to be that guy, I'm okay with it. I'm happy to be that guy. If it leads us to love the Lord more, and to love each other more, and to be more dependent upon God, we're really thankful for the opportunity to go through this.

In all of this, I think we can just praise God. We came into the world with nothing. We're leaving with nothing. The Lord is good. We can praise Him!

We did also want to say thanks to our pastors. I think we are just really blessed to be in a church that preaches the gospel, preaches God's Word, and prepares us for a time like this. We feel well-prepared.

Because the steroids kept Matt from sleeping well, he had been up the night before he spoke to our church, writing out what he would say. Before he spoke that morning, Matt wrote this in his journal:

"God, thank You again for another day. Another day on this earth, God, that I don't deserve. Oh, I wish I woke up like this every day.

"God, I do pray for the pains going on in my body. I don't know what they are, if it's the cancer, but please may they not get worse. God, please help me today to shepherd my family—to feel sorry and be sorrowful where it's good and appropriate, to rejoice where it's good and appropriate, and to just be happy where it's good and appropriate.

"God, please help me to be a loving husband today, a caring father, a faithful friend. I do pray that self-pity would not spring up in my heart. That I really would just believe I don't deserve anything good. Because I don't!

"Please God, may I encourage the body this morning, may I speak words that are truth, please may I magnify You this morning. God, please help us today. Your words, God, truly are so sweet during this time."

Matt had no questions to ask God during this time. Asking "why" or lamenting his situation was simply not a part of his vocabulary.

His journal entries are filled with pleadings of another kind: loving his family and being able to build up the body of Christ.

As I was driving us to church the next morning (Matt couldn't drive, what with all the tumors in his brain), he rehearsed what he was going to say.

As I was wiping away my tears, he reiterated to me sincerely and joyfully that he was happy to go through this trial, to be *that* guy, if God would use it to stir up the body to love the Lord more and each other.

Seeing Matt volunteer himself for such circumstances for the good of the body of Christ so quickly and so joyfully was a remarkable thing. It was Matt, leading by example, running to submit to what the Lord had for him the moment he knew what that was.

January 20, 2017 *(Facebook Update)*

There are many different types of waiting.

Sometimes you wait for a doctor's appointment. Sometimes you wait for a movie to start or a friend to arrive or a new school year to begin. We are waiting for a prognosis on Matt's cancer.

And as we wait, we have seen God provide.

In the eleven days since Matt's MRI, He has provided us a house to live in, our international insurance issues to be worked out (we think!), and a whole bevy of love and support poured out from literally all over the world. It has been a week and a half mixed with so much sorrow and so much joy that most days I alternate between smiling and tears.

What we're waiting for is a confirmed diagnosis and prognosis of Matt's cancer, things like: What kind of lung cancer is it, what would the treatment look like, what is the general life expectancy, etc.

While our long-term future remains uncertain and in God's hands, our immediate future looks like meeting with the neurosurgeon on Wednesday to have Matt's staples from his biopsy removed and discuss the completed pathology. Sometime this week, we should know more of what God has ordained for our earthly future.

While we wait, we trust. Not so much that God will heal Matt-- though that is what we are continuously beseeching Him for should it be His will—but we are trusting that He will use this cancer for His glory and our good.

I suppose some people might respond in anger to a diagnosis like this and that would be understandable. This is hard. In a lot of ways, this week of waiting is probably the easiest week we will have for some time compared to what is coming. And if I thought for one second, that the God who reigns over all things might be giving this to us arbitrarily or punitively, I would be angry, too.

But the God I know, the God of the Bible, does not do things on a whim. He does not roll the dice and watch us scurry out of the way.

He planned the coming of His Son down to the most minute of details—a tied-up donkey, a carpenter named Joseph in the line of David, a census, a greedy friend, a Roman cross. And has that plan that was so painstakingly carried out come to an end? Do the minutia and details no longer matter because Jesus already came and died and rose again?

No, but rather God is still working out His plan because His Son is coming back! Will He take any less care of every single person who lives and breathes and dies now as He did before? He is the sovereign Creator and Sustainer of all things who has planned out all of time and space and history before the dawn of time and He is still working in every single cell and molecule to accomplish His purpose.

He is infinitely wise and working out a plan so majestic and so overwhelmingly good, that He can use terrible things like cancer and death and tragedy and sorrow and sin for good! That any kind of plan of God's would even involve us or benefit us seems incredible. And yet it does. And it springs from a love set upon us before we even loved Him.

There is nothing arbitrary or punitive about this diagnosis. It was given to us by the God who loves us and sent His Son to redeem us from everything truly broken in the world.

If this is how our Lord deems our lives are best used in His plan, we will lay our hands on our mouths and lift up our heads and wait. Wait for the diagnosis to be confirmed. For the prognosis to be laid out.

But most of all, wait for God's plan—whatever it is—to be worked out. For Jesus to come back. For the day promised where there will be no more brokenness and sin and we will get to be with the One who knows us—really knows us—and loves us still.

Unbeknownst to us, a clock was counting down.

Matt was very optimistic that he might have years left; I was, too. But what we couldn't see was that the cancer was gaining enough ground to cause one of the tumors in Matt's brain to bleed again, leading to a stroke.

We thought we had time, so we were making our plans.

We were packing up our things and preparing to move to the house God had so graciously provided for us.

We were picking out new furniture.

Some of the more surreal moments of that whole time were spent inside a furniture store, selecting beautiful, new furniture to go in our beautiful, new house because my husband was dying. Matt would always accompany me, but—cancer or no cancer—he was not thrilled about furniture shopping.

Meanwhile, we were managing side effects.

In cancer, you are constantly treating side effects of drugs meant to off-set the side effects of something else. Because the tumors in Matt's brain were causing swelling, he was given steroids to temporarily reduce it, but after a few days on these, his brain became foggier, and he wasn't always "with it" in the same way.

As always, his primary desire was to honor God and be used by Him.

1/17/2017

"God, thank You for another day. I don't know why You still have me here, but it seems You have me here for one more day. God, what a strange/good/awful situation You have placed us in. I am humbled, and kind of ashamed by some of the grace and kindness we have seen. I don't deserve any gift on this planet from You, God.

"Please teach us how to humbly accept gifts and not cling to things of this world, when we are both losing everything in this world and at the same time getting so much in this world. My heart is tempted to hope in the world, while dying to the world! Please help my fickle heart. God, please really, draw near to me. Help me to see my sin in all of this today.

"God, I do ask for healing, I do ask that I can continue in ministry—but not my will, but yours. You know I would love to come and be with You, but, oh, how sad my wife and kids would be without a husband and father. God, please heal me, send us back to PNG, if it is Your will. God, please help me to make it through this day.

"Please help me to still care well for my wife, and my kids even when I don't feel like quite myself. God, when things get hard, I pray that I can still fight, that I can still grow. Please continue to use us to reach family and friends and proclaim the gospel loudly. Please may I be bold with the gospel today, tomorrow, the rest of the time that I have on this earth!"

1/19/2017

"God, thank You for today. God, please help us every day to honor and glorify You! So many, God, You give suffering to on a daily basis. Really so many have to fight for joy, and even life every day. Thank You for the 36 years where I didn't, oh, how I wished I'd spent them differently!! God, please may I be bold with the gospel today, please may I just think about how everyone is dying, and how they need You. Please use our ransomed lives in any way You choose, and let our song forever be, my only boast is You!"

It was evident that not only was Matt not afraid to die, but he was looking forward to heaven. He wanted to stay for the sake of his wife and kids. But God had made him ready for this time because of his confidence in his hope and inheritance in heaven.

1/20/2017

"God, seeing how You have provided for us has been so amazing. Thank You that I could be used in some way to encourage so many. Thank you, God, it's like a dream to be used by You in this way. Please Lord, continue to use me, continue to use us in all of this. Please may we trust You, may we put our hope in You, please sustain us with Your Word, please uphold us! Thank You that I have another day to live and breathe and be with my family. May I rejoice in this day and rejoice in You.

"Ultimately, God, You are all I need. Please God, do give me more time. I do ask that I would have some more time of fruitful ministry! I ask mostly for the sake of my wife and kids, but I know if You want me home, You'll take care of them, and You'll take care of everyone. Whatever Your will is, God, may it be done, may I just be a humble servant in Your hands!"

My mom graciously volunteered to watch our kids so Matt and I could have an overnight date at a hotel in town.

It would be the last time we would get to do that.

This extended date turned out to be a sweet time of talking to each other and preaching the gospel to each other, reminding each other about what was still true, praying, and reading God's word.

The Lord sent a sweet thunderstorm all through dinner and our hotel stay which was one of our favorite things. (Truth: slightly more Matt's favorite thing than mine, but you learn to love what your spouse loves).

From his journal that day:

1/21/2017

"God, thank You for another day. Thank You that I can sit in this hotel room now with my wife, and we can enjoy a date together. Thank You for the rain, and the wind and whatever the heck is going on outside! Thank You again for using me in this way, God, please continue to use me, use Cameron and her beautiful words.

"Most of all God, please give us joy, please give us hope and peace in all of this. Please may we trust You every step of the way God. May we rejoice in our salvation each day, may we really remember that we deserve nothing on this earth. I deserve wrath today, God. Today is another day where I truly deserve God's wrath because of my sins, and today is another day where I am forgiven all my sins, because of Your great mercy towards me.

"Oh, how I can rest in that every day, no matter the pain or suffering. And yet Lord, I feel I need to more than just rest, and hope and trust—I need to live! I need to care for my kids still, and love my wife well, and serve the body if I can. God, I need to still fight my other besetting sins! And so, I need grace.

"And You know my heart in this as well, God, I pray for survival! I pray I would live, that there would be a miracle! And yet, not my will, but may God's will be done.

"God, please help me to be encouraged and to know You more as I read Your Word now. Thank You also for this time to be awake! Seriously, this is such an added bonus to the steroids. I pray I would have times like this all the way through."

January 25, 2017 *(Facebook Update)*

Today, we were able to learn a bit more about Matt's diagnosis. Here is what we know this week:

--Matt's stage IV lung cancer is confirmed. The subset of lung cancers to which it belongs is adenocarcinoma, a very common type of lung cancer for smokers to get and one of two types that non-smokers can get. In any case, for Matt to be a non-smoker and have this kind of cancer is quite rare.

--The normal prognosis for a 60-year-old smoker with this diagnosis would be 18 months to live. While Matt is certainly not 60 and in otherwise good health, the prognosis for this type and stage of cancer is not typically very good.

Ultimately, though, our hope cannot be in a diagnosis or in a prognosis—in a cutting-edge new treatment or in the skillful hands of a doctor. As the very nice radiation oncologist was explaining things, I just kept thinking that regardless of the outcome of these coming weeks, months, or years, our treasure remains the same. It is not on this earth, but somewhere else entirely. And that is such good news!

Yesterday, after doing some research on lung cancer oncologists and reading the lung cancer facts associated with them, I began to actually accept the fact that Matt might die at the end of this. I had been really trying to guard my heart against doing that prematurely, but yesterday I realized that that possibility was more of a reality than an anxiety.

Matt and I cried in a hallway for about a half an hour and allowed ourselves to grieve over this possibility. There are very real things—four small ones in particular—that Matt will be away from should God choose to take him sooner rather than later and that would be inestimably sad.

But we also know that from there, there really is only good news. Matt is honestly and joyfully looking forward to heaven. And we will see him there soon enough. And more than that---we'll get to see our Savior and be free from a life of sin and fear and brokenness and cancer. One day, the day of death—no matter when it is—will come.

But that day is not today.

Today is the day where we fight to live for those four small things and for the sake of God's glory on this earth.

Today is the day where we ask questions and do research and seek out the best treatment there might be.

We are holding living and dying in both hands right now; fighting to live while simultaneously trusting the Lord with death. And in trusting Him with both those things, there is much joy and peace and hope. Joy in things cancer can never touch, peace in things from which death can never separate us and hope that Matt's life may yet be prolonged here and, if not, that the joy on this earth will be absolutely nothing compared to what's coming.

We also just want to say thank you. The amount of love and prayers and support and meals that have been showered upon us in the last two weeks is bewildering and wonderful. For every person who has texted us or commented on a post or prayed for us or given to us in some way, thank you! We do not deserve it, but are so very comforted by it so thank you, every one of you, for being a part of that. God alone knows what is to come so we are looking to Him. We are in His hands and there we love to be.

It is a gift to be able to say goodbye.

Matt and I had been reluctant to read anything about Stage IV lung cancer until it was a confirmed diagnosis since we didn't want to invite any unnecessary anxiety into our hearts. But we had some guesses on the severity of the situation based on how those around us talked.

Matt wrote in his journal:

1/22/2017

"God, it was a little bit hard for me yesterday to start to realize that probably a lot of people don't think I'm going to make it through this, almost like this is basically the sentence of death. I haven't felt like it's the sentence of death; I've thought this could be an opportunity to be healed and be glorified in that way! And yet, the sad, hard reality is that this could easily end in death. I mean, so many people have come before me with less cancer and have died!

"Yet, I don't actually think this changes anything. It doesn't change how we should think and live and respond. Even if we do find out this is the worst kind of lung cancer there is, it doesn't change Your goodness. Though I may want to fight and continue in ministry with my family and the world, that may not be

Your plan. And oh, it would be nice to come home, but oh so sad for all my family and friends.

"So, I suppose the question is in light of this, what should I do today? How ought I live today? The same I'll live in heaven, the same I'd live without cancer—praising You, worshiping You, knowing You more, fighting my sin, and being bold with the Gospel. Please make me more bold with the gospel, God. Please may I speak oh so much more clearly. And I pray that people will come to know You through this.

"Thank You for yesterday, and the day before, and to be able to spend it with my family. God, please give me grace to spend it well with my family. You know how I feel, the grogginess and cloudiness, oh may I fight through that to still love my wife, and love my kids, and shepherd them, and care well for my family! God, may we speak truth and listen to truth today at church. Please help me to think clearly, to speak rightly and to be an encouragement to my brothers and sisters in Christ!"

Eventually, as the diagnosis seemed more and more likely, we both did some research at separate times on Stage IV lung cancer and came up with the same, terminal conclusion.

Matt wrote:

1/23/2017

"God, I just read a little bit about lung cancer. It looks like the "statistics" are not so good. God, it's crazy for me to think that You could take me home so early, but at the same time, I'm ready to go, too. Of course, I'd like to stay longer, continue the ministry and fight for the spread of the Gospel.

"God, can You just use me in the coming months and years that we have left? I could be only alive for another year, or for another couple years, but I ultimately don't know, and You do know God. God, please provide for us—I know You will—but please may I fight during this time. Even when I don't feel like it, may I eat healthy, exercise, work out my mind, basically everything I need to do to fight this, God!"

After quietly doing my own research, I knew that it was time to talk to Matt and face the reality of our circumstances.

I walked into our friends' house where we were still living and found Matt sitting on the couch. I sat next to him for a while, and we began talking about how bad the diagnosis really was. When we began crying, we moved to the hallway for some privacy.

And sitting there on that wooden floor together, we got to say goodbye.

I was able to tell this man how much I loved him, how he was the best friend I had ever had, what a privilege it had been to be his wife, and how sorry I was for all the time I wasted arguing with him or being selfish.

He said much of the same and then he said something else.

"Cameron," he said with tears in his eyes, "I want to stay for you and for the kids, but honestly, I'm ready to go."

And in those words, there was both heartbreak and hope.

Heartbreak because I knew that my best friend would probably leave me.

And hope—so much hope—because he was not fleeing from death.

He was walking towards it, head lifted high, because he knew where it led.

Matt had been waking up early for the better part of the last two decades and reading his Bible to try to catch a clearer glimpse of his Savior.

And now, the day was in sight where he would finally get to see him face to face.

Death for Matt was not the end.

To the contrary, it was the beginning of everything he had been hoping for, waiting for, and moving across the world for. It meant receiving his inheritance—namely, God! And as much as he loved us, at the end of the day what he loved more than his family was Jesus.

His conversation with that One was similar to the one he had had with me:

"God, I do ask for many more years of life—really for the sake of my family and my friends and whatever ministry You may have me in here. And yet, I'm ready to go home, too. God, please may I honor and glorify You in all of this, be bold with the gospel, and may Your will be done!

"God, I pray that You would use us during this time to preach the gospel, to proclaim Your Word, and to make yourself known. But really every day perhaps the thing that will get me by when my stomach is hurting, or I don't feel myself, is just knowing that You are there with me! God, thank You. I know You love me even still today. I know You care for me right now and this is for my good. It may not actually be that glorious, but it is for my good and the good of the church as well.

"Please may I not lose heart, please give me grace to make it through even this day physically. Thank You for all the kindness through Your people that You have provided."

FEBRUARY

CHAPTER 10

The Clock Runs Out

February 1, 2017 (*Facebook Update*)

Sometimes, I just feel compelled to testify to what God has done these past three weeks.

In the midst of the chaos of all that has happened, we had not even begun to ask questions like where will we live and how when God began answering them.

While we were still reeling from the news of cancer, one of our pastors told us that someone in our church wanted to buy a house we could live in. A few days later, I got a call from a friend who told me that people had stepped forward and wanted to furnish our house for us. We picked out a house on January 17th and it closed on the 25th. When we arrived on moving day last Saturday the 28th, everywhere we looked, there were brand new appliances, furniture, dishes, and bedding. Our fridge and pantry were stocked. Bookcases and beds were already assembled and there was a whole team of people working joyfully to do everything possible to move us in.

Every single one of our needs was met before Matt and I even had to think about it. Who gets to see this kind of kindness? Who gets to see this much of God's goodness on this earth?

My friends, we don't even know who to thank. I have lost count of how many gift cards were handed to us, meals were brought to us, cards and checks were sent to us, arms were wrapped around us, tears were cried with us, and prayers were prayed for us by people we know and people we have never met.

In different circumstances, I would want to sit down with each one and say thank you. I would say we don't deserve this. We are but two sinners in the hands of a good God. We are not the only ones to walk a difficult road, nor will we be the last. But I would say thank you again because we have been so very comforted and loved by every one of these people. So while I might never know or be able to thank everyone, for now, I will give thanks to the One who made each one and moved their heart to love us in this way and at this time because, ultimately, the glory will always go to Him.

If there is faith at all in us, know that the faith and strength come not from us, but from the One who set His great love on us before the foundation of the world; Who gave His Son so that we could be free from our sin and the fear of death.

The news is still bad. The prognosis is still terminal.

But our God is still good. And He is still in control.

He showed His love for us in that while we were still sinners, Christ died for us! We drag our hope back again and again from statistics and new therapies and clinical trials and set them back on that one Rock that will never move, never change, and promises us hope so unbelievable and wonderful, that, if we aren't quite always able to laugh, we are still able to smile.

As that silent clock wound down, we were busy moving.

The speed with which everything happened was God's providential kindness to us as He knew exactly how much time was left on that clock and would make sure we were all moved into our new home by the time it hit zero.

The heaviness of our circumstances was made infinitely lighter by the love we saw poured out by the body of Christ.

Just before move-in day, my mom and I went over to the house and there, like Christmas morning, all over our kitchen countertops sat new *everything*: measuring cups, mixing bowls, a toaster, a KitchenAid stand mixer …anything I could have thought of for a home sat in their carefully arranged boxes. It was our small group, I later learned, who had showered us with love in this way.

On move-in day, Matt and I packed up our few boxes of belongings and went to the house, only to see everything was already done for us.

New beds assembled. New dishes washed and put away in our cupboards. Bookshelves set up and filled with books. Toys for the kids, organized bins and food neatly stocked in our fridge and pantry.

A small army from our church and beyond had been marching in and out of our house all day long, bewildering our new neighbors with the sheer number of people helping to move us in.

There was no need too big or too small for our fellow Christians to fill.

Multiple families stepped forward to adopt our kids into their homeschools so that they might continue to have some structure and stability in their days.

There was a steady stream of meals dropped off—something that would continue for the next six months.

Someone was there to fix our car free of charge, clean our pool free of charge, clean our house, buy our groceries. The list was endless.

We were weeping in this season, but we were not weeping alone.

We were surrounded by God's love in a thousand ways expressed through the servant-hearted hands and feet of His people.

In Psalm 50:10, the LORD declares that He owns the cattle on a thousand hills. His provision for us during this time was so abundant, so unnecessarily extravagant, that it was almost as if He were saying, "See all that I have done? Can I not do all things? If I wanted to remove this illness from Matt, could I not do just that? If it remains then, it is clearly My will."

Yes, God had laid a heavy burden upon us, but He knew exactly how much strength it would require to carry it and provided many hands and feet of not just our church, but churches all over Phoenix, all over the United States, all over the world, to help us carry it.

If Matt and I were overwhelmed by anything in these days, it was by the kindness of God through His people.

Matt wrote:

"God, it's Sunday morning! I'm looking forward to going to church this morning, Lord. Thank You for this day. Thank You that I can sit here in this living room that someone else has provided and talk to You!

"Thank You for providing for our family, for caring for us in this tangible way—it is truly amazing to see what You have done. God, You know my heart. You don't even need to use anything, You could just heal me! And yet, not what I will but may Your will be done. You have better plans than me, God, and if those plans are for me to die next week or next month or next year, then may I rest in them and trust You. After all, we're all going to die eventually.

"Thank You for saving me God, you really didn't have to, but You saved this punk kid. What hope, what joy I have now, and I do want to see You face to face!

"Ahhh, but here I am in this state where I am not with You, I don't know how long I'll live, and I'm not 100% healthy. This is where my battle is, this is where I need grace,

"God, to fight my sin, to be content today, and to glorify You with my life today. Please help me to love my wife, love my kids, love our church. Please give us wisdom in the coming months about what our lives should look like, God. Thank You for your Word—please use Your Word to grow me and that I might know You more God!"

Still unafraid of death, Matt began building a theology as each day passed on how to live in light of a terminal diagnosis:

"God, thank You for another day. Thank You that I feel like myself right now in this moment! Thank You for this house, God, thank You for my wife— for the immense grace You are showing her.

"God, please help me to make it through this. Why? I mean, I think ultimately for the sake of my family, for the sake of ministry, for the sake of the body. But maybe I can glorify You more in my death than in my life?

"God, may Your will be done, just use me in all of this—I don't want to waste a day of it. Please may I grow each day, seek You each day and worship You each day. God, thank You for loving me, for sending Jesus to die for me, thank You for saving me. Please may I trust You today, may I be diligent today,

and may I fight to love my wife and love my kids and love the body and be bold with the Gospel today! Help me now as I read Your Word God to know You more!"

The reality of how eight years of preparation and labor for the gospel in Papua New Guinea might be gone began to sink in around this time. Just a month before, that was our whole life, and now it seemed as if our role in that was over.

Matt wrote:

2/1/2017

"God, thank You for another day where I can sit here and talk to You! God, this life is so strange. I'm still close to death, I mean, I have death—cancer—raging inside of me trying to kill me, and yet there is this hope of living a little longer. Perhaps this will just bring us back to PNG?

"It's just crazy to think the ministry will be gone, but maybe You have another ministry for us, maybe You have something better for us to do here. Either way, God, we still know You. You still love us, You still care for us. It's so funny, I'm less concerned about how I should die and more concerned now about how I should live!"

As we settled into our new house and circumstances, we began to wade through the waters of oncologists and treatment options. In a city the size of Phoenix, the options were overwhelming.

We desperately wanted to find the one doctor who would not only be competent in treating Matt, but also truly invested in him.

But how would we find an oncologist like that?

Turns out, we wouldn't have to.

God brought him to us.

After several recommendations for the same doctor, we scheduled an appointment with an oncologist named Dr. Clayton Polowy.

It was February 1st.

Matt would have a stroke in less than 24 hours.

And in God's providence, it would be the extraordinary efforts of this doctor that would make the difference between life and death for Matt in the coming weeks.

Matt, at this point, was really struggling with functionality. His brain was foggy from being on the steroids for so long, but he also had a headache.

One of the tumors in his brain had begun to bleed again and the pressure the excess fluid was slowly putting on his brain was building.

We were Dr. Polowy's last appointment of the day.

Matt really wasn't himself at this appointment, but Dr. Polowy sat and talked with us for over an hour. It turns out, he had had another young, non-smoking patient with Stage IV lung cancer years ago whose name also happened to be Matt, and about whom he had cared deeply.

He felt connected to us, and before we left his office, he gave each of us his personal cell phone number, along with the peace of mind that somehow, in the vast sea of oncologists, God had led us to one who cared about us.

Who knew how long and how many pieces God had moved prior to this day to bring Dr. Polowy into our lives?

We went to sleep that night with thankful hearts and new plans.

And then, the clock ran out.

*　　　　*　　　　*　　　　*

I woke up from a nightmare.

It was 5:00 in the morning, and I would normally just go back to sleep, but the nightmare had been so vivid and scary that I got out of bed to find Matt. As usual, Matt was awake before me, reading his Bible on the couch.

I began to tell him all about my nightmare but stopped when I noticed his face.

"What's wrong?" I asked.

"I just feel really weird," he said. "My head feels strange, and I keep leaning to the left when I walk."

Immediately, my heart began to race.

Matt was not an alarmist.

I knew that if he was saying there was something wrong, there was definitely something wrong.

He told me he had gone to bed with a headache the night before and had been unable to sleep because his stomach was also hurting. Since then, the headache had only gotten worse.

His journal entry from that unnerving morning reads:

2/2/2017

"God, it's me—I don't feel so great. I just want to cast that anxiety upon you, my head hurting slightly, my stomach issues that kept me up most of the night. God, I feel like these steroids are going to take me out before I make it to any surgery or anything. I do feel a little off, and I wonder if it's in my head literally.

"God, please sustain me. YOU are in control of the cancer; You can keep it at bay, or YOU can let it grow. Please keep it at bay so it can be taken care of by the gamma knife radiation or the drugs. Again, God, I ask that there would be a mutation and I can take the targeted therapy, that just seems like a good option. But if chemo is the only road, then may You use whatever road we take to heal me. I do pray You would heal me of this and use me in ministry somewhere. Really anything could happen, God. I pray that You would sustain me. May I not have any seizures or anything in the coming weeks, but may I be able to last.

"I hope this is just because I am tired or something that I am moving so slow. God, thank You for another day, though. May I live this day to Your glory. Please again make me bold with the gospel, and may I love my wife and kids the best I can today.

"Please may my head stop hurting. God, may I just think much about the glories that are coming—seeing You in all Your glory, what a glorious day that will be! Thank You for saving me, God. I am truly saved from all my sins by Your grace. Truly, my biggest problem is solved. If I were to die now, I would be in eternal life and joy only by Your mercy and grace.

135

"And so, I don't fear death, God, and yet I grieve for those left behind. I'd like to stay for their sake, to continue as a father and husband and friend. Please may I make every effort to fight God!"

As Matt continued to describe his symptoms, my whole body began to shake. I had no idea what a stroke or a seizure was, but I was pretty sure one of those things was happening to my husband.

Our kids were still sleeping, so we called my mom to take Matt to the emergency room.

When Matt was first diagnosed, as unexpected and bad as the news had been, I still felt steady enough to handle it.

But as I watched Matt struggle to put his jeans on that morning, leaning to the left and losing his balance, I was, for the first time, honest-to-goodness scared of what was happening.

As we waited for my mom to arrive, we prayed together.

During his prayer, Matt kept pausing in really unnatural places.

When he was done, he said again, "I just feel really weird."

With each passing minute, he seemed to be less coordinated in his speech and movement, heightening our sense that something was really wrong.

My mom arrived, having run every red light as safely as she could, and they were off.

In the quiet of the house, I sat, praying, and trying to calm down. I called a dear friend of mine who came over and prayed with me as I waited to hear what was going on.

The phone rang.

Matt was having a hemorrhagic stroke in his brain. The tumor that was bleeding was spilling blood into and around the right side of his brain, causing swelling and pressure, damaging cells and tissue, and causing the loss of function.

His situation was critical.

A friend graciously volunteered to stay with our still-sleeping kids as I headed to the hospital.

Meanwhile, in the emergency room, Matt got a call.

It was Dr. Polowy, the oncologist from the day before, calling to see how Matt was doing—completely unaware of what was happening.

Matt said that he was fine, but that he did happen to be in the ER and that there was a strong possibility he was having a stroke.

They were interrupted as Matt had to get off the phone, but Dr. Polowy was now looped into the situation—a fact that would prove critical in the days to come.

By the time I got to the hospital, Matt's condition had deteriorated.

In addition to losing more mobility on his left side, he was now crying uncontrollably.

As the pressure on Matt's motor strip from the bleeding intensified, Matt lost the ability to control his emotions.

Having only seen Matt cry a handful of times in our whole marriage, this new development added fuel to my already present fear.

Later, the damage from the stroke would have the opposite effect—causing Matt to temporarily have no emotions at all—but today, Matt could not stop crying.

"I don't know why I'm crying," Matt began, before I was even through the curtains of his ER cubicle. "I'm not scared."

I grabbed hold of that hand I had been holding for the last decade.

"I'm not afraid to die," he assured me again, looking me in the eye, tears rolling down his cheeks. "I'm just sorry it's going down like this."

I nodded, crying with him, aware that today might be the day the Lord called Matt home.

We said goodbye to each other one more time.

Matt's situation was emergent, but in God's providence, there wouldn't be a bed available for about an hour at Barrow Neurological, where he needed to have surgery.

So, instead of a helicopter, an ambulance was called.

By the time the EMTs came to load Matt on a stretcher, he had lost the ability to walk. They transferred him to a gurney and then to the ambulance.

Matt kept apologizing the whole way through, something he would continue to do with every medical professional whenever they asked him to do something that he was unable to do. He also made sure to thank each and every nurse or doctor with whom he came into contact.

I climbed into the ambulance with him and proceeded to drive the 30 minutes across town at 25 miles per hour.

No siren. No changing lanes. We didn't even speed.

It was rush hour in Phoenix and we were stuck in traffic, while my husband lay dying from a stroke.

Every time we would move forward a few feet and then stop, I had to trust God all over again. I got to a place in that ambulance where I realized that if God wanted Matt to die because there was no bed for him at Barrow or because of rush hour traffic, I could trust Him with that.

Matt didn't waste that ambulance ride.

Though having a stroke and slowly becoming paralyzed on his left side, Matt hadn't lost his sense of humor, or his desire to proclaim Christ. There he was in that ambulance, joking around with me about paralysis and strokes one minute and then turning and sharing the gospel with the EMT beside us the next.

Matt's friend, Jake, called while we drove.

Matt, holding the phone with his right hand, just reiterated how this, too, was the Lord's will, and we could trust Him.

Finally, after turtles and sloths had lapped us several times, we arrived at Barrow to an available room.

An emergency hemorrhage evacuation procedure was scheduled at 2 p.m. to suction as much of the blood off Matt's brain as possible.

Meanwhile, Matt's body continued to shut down. His speaking ability became impaired. When he began vomiting in his pre-op MRI because of the pressure on his brain, they had to partially sedate him.

When 2 p.m. finally rolled around, a nurse arrived to lead Matt and I to the surgery room.

We were led through a maze of hospital hallways and elevators, finally stopping at a crossroads of new hallways, with a pair of stark, double doors directly in front of us. I signed form after form that basically said it was fine if Matt died, while Matt looked on, unable to sign, from the bed on which he lay. When I had signed the last form, I told Matt I loved him through tears, really not sure if I would ever see him again on this earth.

The flurry of activity and nurses that had accompanied us down into this place suddenly disappeared as he was whisked through the double doors.

There I stood, without even my guide nurse, tears still falling down my face.

Matt was gone, perhaps permanently.

I had no idea where I was.

And I was alone.

But when I did not even know where I was, God knew.

Someone suddenly appeared near me, and, when I turned, there stood Smedly, our pastor.

My only question was, "*How?*"

He said something about pulling a clergy card, but all I really heard was that I wasn't alone in that moment.

I was so thankful to have someone there, walking next to me during the long, silent trek back to Matt's empty ICU room.

Again, we waited for the results of a brain surgery.

Again, we waited for Dr. Francisco Ponce to tell us Matt's fate.

But there were no light-hearted stories or film reviews during this waiting. There was instead earnest prayer and dependence on God.

The surgery was successful.

Although the most immediate threat to Matt's life was removed, his battle to survive had just begun. Because recovering from the stroke was now the top priority, we could not treat the cancer in his body, allowing the tumors in his body and brain to grow unchecked.

The threats were real, and, in the days following, many would come crashing down on us.

But Matt was still alive.

When I look at the situation, right in the thick of it, I see God's kindness on that day: in the doctors and nurses He provided to care for us at two different hospitals, in a room that did eventually become available, in an emergency surgery performed by a doctor we knew, in a friend to walk beside me when I otherwise would have walked alone, and in Matt surviving the stroke.

But God's kindness was actually much bigger.

Because here's the thing.

We should not have even been in Phoenix on February 2nd, 2017.

We should have been in a remote, helicopter-access-only village in Papua New Guinea.

We should have been thousands of miles away from any decent medical care, let alone a special neurological hospital.

Had Susanna not gotten strep throat all those times to the extent she did, we would never have come home when we did.

In fact, had Onesimus not woken up that morning with his second case of strep, it would have just been Susanna and I coming home.

Matt would have had symptoms in the village, but they were so vague and inconsistent, they never would have warranted us paying for a helicopter ride and two plane flights out of the country just to get an MRI.

Without God's intervening grace, Matt should have had a stroke on February 2nd and died on that mountain without us having a clue as to what had happened.

Instead, here we were, with family and friends and medical care that saved his life.

And Onesimus never got strep again.

We live in a fallen world with hard things.

But oh, for the one who has God as his refuge and strength! That one knows that though he does not know the future, God does! And He promises to work all things for the good of those who love Him.

Our Facebook post from the day of the stroke read as follows:

February 2, 2017 *(Facebook Update)*

Just a quick update at the end of an unexpected and difficult day.

Early this morning, Matt began having stroke-like symptoms (leaning to the left while walking, difficulty speaking, pressure in the back of his head, etc.) which prompted us to get him to the ER. Once there, a CT scan revealed bleeding on the right frontal lobe of his brain which was putting intense pressure on the motor strip of his brain. Over the next 8 hours, Matt lost nearly all movement on the left side of his body. He went into surgery around 2:00pm where the neurosurgeon drained as much of the blood off his brain as he could.

Matt is stable in the ICU, but still without any function on the left side of his body. Time will tell if this is a long-term effect.

What this means for the road ahead of him is not yet determined, although we know we are now dealing with a stroke and stage IV lung cancer. Before he lost the ability to speak very clearly, Matt just kept saying that he loved me and that he was in no way scared about what was happening—only sad for me.

Today was a hard day.

Before today, Matt and I were actively and jointly fighting this battle side-by-side. Now, we are still fighting together, but he is fighting his battle much more quietly and my role in this fight has shifted.

Watching him lose function both physically and cognitively throughout the day was possibly one of the most difficult things I have witnessed. I kept telling him that I was okay; that I was happy and he needed to know that. And I meant every word of it every time. If this is where God has me, then it is a good place to be and I am happy to be there even while it is also a sorrowful place.

In the next few days, we'll watch and pray for no re-bleeding in his brain. We'll pray that treatment for the cancer would not be delayed by this stroke and that movement might return to the left side of his body.

Pray for our kids who will no doubt try to process this the best way they know how and for those who are with them to love them well while we're in the hospital. And pray that God's glory might still be declared in us, though it might not be expressed through Matt in words for a time.

We look forward to the day when our tongues will be loosed from every shackle to sing the praises of our God with uninterrupted and inexhaustible energy. When we will behold our Savior and no longer have any desire to wonder why His plans are so different from ours with its suffering, and to wonder instead at His immeasurable sacrifice for our sins, to marvel and worship at his suffering for us.

Until that day comes, though, we will fix our eyes on Jesus, the author and finisher of our faith, Who for the joy set before him, endured the cross, despising the shame, and is set down at the right hand of the throne of God.

CHAPTER 11

Our Hope is in Him and Him Alone

February 6, 2017 (*Facebook Update*)

There is a battle being fought in Matt's hospital room.

A week ago, the battle looked daunting, but somewhat one-dimensional with the attack coming from one direction: stage IV lung cancer. Today, the battle is multi-dimensional and it seems as though every few hours, there is a new attack from a different direction. But there are also sweet reprieves and glimpses of hope along the way.

Here's the update: In the good news department, Matt was able to move the fingers on his left hand yesterday and squeeze with it. Some of the best of the good news is Matt's communication ability. Since the bleed happened in the part of the brain that controls emotions, Matt isn't actually able to express any emotions--his voice is monotone and his face and eyes look vacant. So he tries extra hard in his words to make all of us know he's still the same inside. He makes the same jokes and says things that regular, joyful Matt would say. He's also speaking more in phrases and sentences, which has been wonderful.

His obstacles, however, tend to overcome those bright spots. It goes like this: Matt has cancer; the cancer is consuming Matt's blood in such a way that he has lost the ability to clot wounds normally. He is in critical condition.

There is hope from a medical standpoint, in that Matt tested positive for a gene mutation called ALK which makes him a candidate for a targeted therapy drug that, if he responds to it, might be able to control the cancer for some months, possibly granting Matt the ability to fight through this. The goal right now is to keep Matt stable until we can get that drug.

The last few days have been difficult.

I feel like I have a pretty good theology about how to live, and a pretty good theology about how to die. But I don't really have one for this in-between place—this place where life and death meet so closely, where machines alarm and nurses rush in and you hold your breath. But I'm building one as I go, and it looks a lot like trusting the Lord, casting my anxieties on Him because He cares for me and for Matt.

It also looks like hoping. I realized yesterday that it was easier for me to prepare for Matt's death than to hope for his life because hope can be so acutely painful when disappointed. But the Bible tells me that love hopes all things. And if Matt can fight to breathe and swallow then I can surely fight to hope and hope fiercely until God says otherwise.

God has been faithful to uphold us even in the midst of this. Matt is not scared or sad; he's still quite himself, albeit he can't speak the same way, and that in and of itself has been such a kindness of God to me.

Ultimately, when Matt and I say to each other 'it's going to be okay', it's a true statement because God has not changed. His goodness has not changed. Our salvation has not changed. Though our hearts have been wrenched and wrung here these past few days and we don't yet know what God has planned for us, our hope is still in Him and in Him alone.

Matt was completely paralyzed on his left side.

He could feel sensation on the left side of his body—and that was a good sign! But he could not move it at all.

He could not eat. He could not drink.

He had no expression in his face. In addition to the paralysis, Matt woke up from the stroke with no emotions.

I didn't even know it was possible to lose your emotions, but it is. And for someone as gregarious and outgoing and joyful as Matt, this was a jarring change.

He could not smile or frown. He could not laugh or cry. His tone was completely without expression.

He would tell me later he simply felt nothing inside.

The most disturbing part of the paralysis was Matt's face.

His normally laughing, crinkling blue eyes had been replaced by pupils devoid of expression. His always-present smile had been replaced by flaccid cheeks and a limp mouth. There was not so much as a wrinkle in his brow or a turn of his lip.

He just looked vacant.

I wasn't sure if the stroke had changed his personality at all since he wasn't able to communicate much.

That is, until the bronch cart incident.

A nurse managing another patient poked his head into Matt's room to see if he could borrow a bronch cart (a portable bronchoscopy), to which Matt's nurse responded that she still needed it. There was a moment of nurse tension and then he left.

It was at this point that poor, flaccid-face Matt said, "Get your own bronch cart!"

On paper, this may not seem all that funny.

But in that moment, it was hilarious.

It had to have been in the top ten jokes made by a stroke victim in a neuro ICU.

Sure, his timing might have been a bit off what with having a stroke and all, but it was clever, it was funny, *it was Matt.*

Inside, I breathed a sigh of relief and a prayer of thanks to God.

As the hours marched on, the biggest unknown was how permanent the paralysis was. If movement is going to come back at all after a stroke, it usually tends to come back within a few days.

And in God's kindness, that is exactly what happened. The day he moved his left thumb on command was the best day because it was indicative that he might get it all back!

Unfortunately, paralysis and stroke recovery were the least of Matt's problems.

Because the cancer that had caused them in the first place was still growing unchecked.

And once again, it was gaining ground.

We were helpless to treat it with Matt in his present condition. But we knew that if we didn't do something, it was likely he wouldn't make it out of the ICU.

Before the stroke, we had been eagerly awaiting the results of the genetic testing on the tumor from the biopsy to see if Matt might be a candidate for targeted therapy.

I knew that we could not do anything until we got those results but, not being a part of the medical world, I had no idea how to get those answers.

But the Lord did.

After his phone call with Matt, Dr. Polowy had continued to follow his case. He had tracked down the results from the genetic testing and, as soon as he saw that Matt was a candidate for the targeted therapy drug, he called me personally to let me know.

This was great news!

But the obstacles in getting the drug to him were significant.

For one, Matt would have to recover enough to take the medicine, most likely pills that could not be put through his feeding tube, and he was nowhere near being able to swallow water yet, let alone a pill.

Secondly, this form of targeted therapy (called Alectinib) was not yet FDA-approved. That meant that there would be a fight to prove that Matt needed it badly enough to bypass the more traditional, FDA-approved drugs. This also meant that someone in the medical world with more knowledge than me would need to be willing to take on that fight.

Because Matt was being treated at Barrow and had an assigned oncologist there, we were not under the care of Dr. Polowy; meaning, he could not get the medication for us.

But he could talk to the doctor who could.

The day after Matt's stroke, test results in hand, Dr. Polowy left a voicemail for our oncologist at Barrow. He sent him the testing results and pathology and encouraged him to get the Alectinib for Matt.

He did not receive a response.

He let me know he had sent the information over, but that I might need to advocate for the drug when I saw the doctor.

Patient advocacy is not a spectator sport.

There came a day where I realized that it wasn't the doctors or the nurses who knew the whole picture about Matt; it was me. And if I didn't advocate for what I knew he needed, he would not get it.

That morning I knew that my fight was to talk to the Barrow oncologist about Alectinib.

And the odds looked long.

What did I know about cancer?

What did I know about targeted therapy?

Somehow, I was going to have to convince this very busy man to get this non-FDA-approved drug for Matt and to take on a fight for a patient he didn't know. I knew that God was sovereign and that all I could really do was ask.

As it turned out, I wouldn't have to.

As I was gathering my notes and courage, our oncologist walked in.

Brusque, but kind, he said, "So, I received the genetic testing results showing that Matt has the ALK mutation from a Dr. Polowy—do you know him?"

Having heard him just steal my opening line, I nodded.

He then explained how after receiving Dr. Polowy's message, he had begun the process of getting the Alectinib.

Not an easy process, he assured us. There were significant hurdles in the way.

But his office—specifically, his assistant, Sherry—was the best in the business. If there was anyone we wanted on the frontlines of that fight, it would be her.

By his best estimation, Matt should have the medicine within five days.

Oh, and the drug would be free for a year.

He left the room as briskly as he had entered it.

My mom and I looked at each other, speechless.

God didn't need my notes.

He didn't need my persuasive arguments—my ethos, my logos, my pathos. Proverbs 21:1 says that "the king's heart is a stream of water in the hand of the Lord; he turns it wherever he will."

Some days, God gave me strength to fight the battles.

Others, He fought for me.

For God to provide someone who wasn't even our official oncologist to go out of his way and contact another oncologist—something that isn't traditionally done—to advocate on our behalf was already remarkable.

But to have the person not only listen to such advice, but expedite his action on it? And then to have such an expensive and experimental drug come at no cost to us?

Only the Lord can do such things.

It was a miracle in and of itself.

But we would soon need another one.

Because in order for Matt to begin taking Alectinib, he had to stay alive long enough for us to get it.

February 9, 2017 *(Facebook Update)*

The biggest physical challenges Matt faces today and for which I know he would dearly love prayer are his thirst and his restlessness. Because his swallowing muscles were impaired by the stroke, Matt hasn't been able to have a proper drink of water in seven days. Although he is getting plenty of IV fluids, he is still very thirsty. In addition, because he is unable to move the limbs on the left side of his body, the limbs on his right rove and search restlessly all day long. It's a bit like involuntary flailing. It is exhausting for Matt and nearly non-stop.

Today, in the midst of the flailing and the thirst, Matt looked at me and said, "This is exactly what the Lord wants for us."

And, look, it is not easy.

Sometimes life isn't because we live in a broken world where instead of running to God with nothing in our hands but surrender and pleas of mercy, we adamantly insist on clinging to the broken shards

of our own good works or our pithy arguments with God. In only one of those scenarios is there life and life abundantly.

A long time ago, Matt and I agreed with God that our lives and our deaths belonged to Him, that He alone was our treasure. In His hands, if you have eyes to see it, are life and kindness and mercy and love purchased at the cost of His Son in the midst of a world starving for such things. And so it is that we still say that today is the day that the Lord has made—struggles and all—and we will rejoice and be glad in Him.

Matt was in the ICU for fourteen days.

It was a traumatizing place to be.

The sounds were traumatizing. If it wasn't Matt's machines alarming, it was someone else's.

The sights were traumatizing. The skull of the patient next door to Matt had clearly been crushed by something.

After doing my best to "sleep" in the ICU for a few nights, I knew that it wasn't sustainable. There were four kids who needed to see at least one of their parents every once in a while.

One of Matt's friends kindly set up an Excel spreadsheet with a rotation of kind, godly, selfless men who would stay the night with Matt so that I could sleep at home with the kids.

In total, Matt was in the hospital for sixty days.

He did not sleep alone for a single night.

Once again, God answered with not just one friend or two—but with an abundance of brothers in Christ, who gave up the comforts of their own home and families for a night (or multiple nights!) so I could sleep at home with mine.

Every morning, I would get off the elevator on the 4th floor at Barrow, walk past the Bret Michaels Music and Hospitality room, and breathe the same prayer: "*Mercy*".

I knew I didn't deserve to *not* walk through this. I knew that what I deserved because of my sins was so much worse than what I was dealing with. This new day, even with all its difficulty, was still mercy. I breathed this prayer for mercy every morning for sixty days.

And God answered it every single time.

With the ups and downs of these days in the ICU, I would often say that my thoughts were like wild horses—threatening to drag me off to every new possibility of the worst possible outcome. It took all the self-control I had to rein them in each day, to deal with the situation at hand, and not be anxious about the "what-ifs" of tomorrow.

These were hard days for me, but they were much harder for Matt.

The flailing described in the post was difficult to watch. The thirst was just as bad.

Matt could not swallow water or any fluid without aspirating (breathing it into his lungs). His body was hydrated with IV fluids, but his mouth was incessantly parched.

Watching Matt suffer in these ways was painful, even excruciating at some points.

But still, we weren't alone in the ICU.

One night, several nurses came into Matt's room and began thanking me for the gift of pizza and salad that had just arrived. Bewildered, I told them I had no idea what they were talking about.

It turned out that a kind friend ordered pizza and salad for the *entire floor* of ICU nurses just to say thank you for taking care of Matt.

My family and Matt's family were a constant source of strength.

My mom was an ever-present friend and pillar of support. Matt's sister and mom and aunt were near. The rest of Matt's family—his dad, stepmom, and brother—lived in Louisiana.

When they heard about the stroke, Matt's dad, Richard, and brother, Blake, flew out to see him. It was a difficult time to visit Matt, as he was still in the early stages of recovering from the stroke, still without emotions and not able to communicate very much. But still, he was awake, and they were able to visit and talk with him.

I talked to Richard, outside of the ICU ward and listened to him talk about how much he loved his son.

We said goodbye, and they flew back to Louisiana.

Matt's situation was still precarious, but thus far death had been kept at bay.

But Matt was not the only person in the world.

We did not know it, but death would indeed touch us in the coming days in a way we could have never predicted.

CHAPTER 12

Not Giving Us More Than We Can Bear

February 13, 2017 *(Facebook Update)*

Matt's blood continues to be problematic as he is having to be transfused every 24 hours. He also still does not have the use of his left shoulder, arm, hand, and leg. He cannot walk or stand by himself; cannot eat or drink or speak easily. My husband, the funniest man I know, the man with a smile for everything and everyone, cannot physically laugh or smile yet. And then, of course, there is the cancer— a battle in and of itself without the added damage from the stroke. And so we pray.

In addition, we received another piece of bad news yesterday.

1 Corinthians 10:13 promises us that God will never give us a temptation or a test beyond what we can endure. We held to that promise yesterday morning when we received a phone call informing us that Matt's dad, Richard, passed away.

This phone call was especially jarring given the fact that he had just been with us visiting Matt in the hospital not many days ago. Having to deliver this news to Matt on top of what he was already working through was not easy.

Yet to this also, Matt's response again was, "It's okay. This is the Lord's will. I'm glad I got to see him." Matt loved his dad and his dad loved Matt. Our hearts are grieved for his wife and the rest of his family as they, too, mourn this loss.

What God has given us seems like a lot and it is.

And yet, I have been encouraged in the last day or two by the thought that God is still worthy to be praised. Regardless of our circumstances, this holds true. If we did not sing His praises, the very rocks would cry out because He is that good and worthy and eternal and holy. There is a danger in the myopic tendency that comes with being in such dire straits. The temptation to let the practical implications of this diagnosis and stroke—as overwhelming and sad as they are true—rule my thoughts and heart each day is real.

And there is a version of this story where I let lamenting over what has been lost lead me down a road of bitterness or resentment over what still remains; where I exchange gratitude for complaining, joy for constant, unproductive weeping. For the sake of the gospel, for the sake of my own soul, I cannot take that road.

The day that I think the lapping waves of my present sorrow outweigh the everlasting ocean of eternal joy, the day that I think that this light and momentary affliction which our good Father has given us can in some way compare to the eternal weight of glory purchased by God's Son on our behalf through His own redeeming suffering, that is the day that this battle has truly been lost. And even then, it can still be won by remembering.

What we're going through is hard and real and the implications of it need to be faced and dealt with. But we do not face them alone and they will never be meaningless or without absolute purpose.

So, we press on and we still sing. We sing the praises of the One who made us and saved us. We sing of the One who is sustaining Matt in that hospital bed as I write. And we sing of the One who will one day—despite all our sin—grant us an eternity of doing just that.

I was standing in my kitchen, getting ready to head to the hospital, when my phone rang.

It was Jill, Matt's sister, calling to tell me that Matt's dad, Richard, had passed away. No one was sure exactly what had happened. He hadn't been feeling well and had gone to the hospital only to be sent home. He went back a few hours later and died shortly after arrival.

I had no words.

Richard had just been out here; I had just spoken to him.

My heart broke for Matt's family with all that they were having to go through.

How would I tell Matt?

In the midst of all he had already lost, how would I tell him he had also lost his dad?

I originally thought of waiting until he was stronger and more alert, but when I got to the hospital that day, I couldn't *not* tell him.

With shaking hands, I took a deep breath.

"Matt, I have some bad news."

Matt's eyes went wide—an activity I hadn't seen since the stroke.

"Who else has cancer?" he asked.

"No one," I assured him, my heart aching that this was the first thing he thought of. "Your sister called this morning and…Matt, she told me that your dad passed away yesterday."

Matt would tell me later that when I told him this news, he felt no sadness inside because his emotions were still not present. He could only take it in as information. But this he did still through the lens of Scripture.

"It's okay," he said. "This is the Lord's will. I'm glad I got to see him."

There was not much time to mourn because Matt's situation was becoming more and more critical.

The hope all along was that Matt's body would hold off the cancer long enough to give the medicine a chance to work, although there was no guarantee that it would.

But this was a battle that he was beginning to lose.

The cancer was slowly and surely killing him.

Every day his labs were dropping more and more outside of normal bounds. Transfusions that Matt had been relying on to keep his blood stable were becoming necessary more and more frequently.

As it turned out, Matt had developed low-grade DIC (disseminated intravascular coagulation)—a serious condition where the clotting factors in the blood become overactive, forming small blood clots throughout the body's blood vessels that inevitably leads to internal bleeding. But the only way to treat DIC is to treat the underlying cause of it, which we knew in this case to be the cancer.

The day came where the Alectinib—that life-saving medicine for Matt—arrived, but there was a problem.

The pills could not be crushed and given to Matt through his feeding tube.

He would have to swallow them.

In order to do that, he first had to pass his swallowing test with the speech pathologist—a test which he had already failed multiple times at this point, coughing whenever he tried to swallow liquid.

Now, as his wife, I knew that Matt was a cougher. Something about his esophagus ever since I had met him had just made him a guy who coughed a lot.

I was no medical professional, and I had no desire to see my husband aspirate, but I did ask/beg/plead for the speech pathologist to do a video swallowing exam to make sure.

She agreed.

He swallowed the liquid and coughed as he had in the other tests.

But against all odds, and to the disbelief of the administering speech pathologist, there was no aspiration happening—the man just liked to cough!

He passed the swallowing test and was officially approved to take his pills.

As it turned out, it wasn't just one little pill that Matt had to take the next day.

It was four. Really, four of the biggest pills I had ever seen.

No speech pathologist, I believe, would have advised someone who had just passed their swallowing test *the day before* to be downing big pills in applesauce, but we were out of options.

I sat across from Matt, looked him in his expressionless eyes, and took a deep breath.

"Matt, if there was any other way for us to get these into your system, we would do it. There is no other way. You have to either swallow these pills or you will most likely die. Do you think you can do it?"

He nodded.

If you have never known someone who has lost much of their swallowing function, it might be hard to see why this was so difficult. But the amount of coordination required for a man who just started swallowing things yesterday to swallow a large pill like that was like asking a half-drowning man to breathe air.

But one thing that I knew about my husband was that if it was possible for him to do it, he would do it.

We prayed, and then I picked up the applesauce, with speech pathologists and nurses standing nearby.

He just focused on me, I put the pill in the applesauce and counted with him for a good swallow.

He did it.

It was, like, miracle number 487 at this point.

He swallowed that pill, and then the next, and then the next, and then the next.

He was exhausted when he was done, but we were ecstatic.

We had no promise that those pills would even do anything, but oh! If they could, they were at least in his system now.

And so we kept transfusing Matt. He kept taking his pills.

And we waited.

We had gotten him the Alectinib.

The only question was, had we gotten it to him in time?

February 18, 2017 *(Facebook Update)*

"You have heard of the steadfastness of Job, and you have seen the purpose of the Lord, how the Lord is compassionate and merciful" (James 5:11).

When I read this verse, I think mostly of the second half. I think of the two statements given here: 1) that God has a purpose, and 2) that He is compassionate and merciful. I think how God has a purpose for

each one of us, without exception, and how the primary observation of James here when he comments on the life of Job, which was marked so emphatically by suffering, is God's compassion; His mercy. I would say, too, that this has been my primary observation of the last few weeks in what He has purposed for us. God is compassionate, He has not given us more than we can bear with His help. And He is merciful; we are still not getting what we deserve.

By far, the biggest development in the last three days has been Matt's blood numbers (his platelets, his fibrinogen, etc.). These had been trending downward since his stroke, leading to a diagnosis of low-grade DIC, a condition wherein the clotting factors in your blood become overactive. This condition does not happen on its own, but always has an underlying cause; in this case, cancer. I explain all of this to let you know that three days ago, those numbers for Matt began coming up. For three days in a row now, without any transfusions, Matt's platelets, fibrin levels, and red blood cells have come up to almost normal levels.

This is significant because it seems to point to the fact that the drug Matt is taking is working, that he is responding to it, that we are, in fact, treating the underlying cause--the cancer. This is such a kindness from God!

Matt also continues to develop movement in his left hand, another thing for which we are thankful this week. Maybe next week it will be his arm or shoulder or leg, but for today, we are thankful for his hand.

Along with treating the systemic cancer in his body, Matt also began whole brain radiation this week. It was a victory in the sense that he made it to this point, but on that day, it felt much like a loss. With the radiation, there is a chance that Matt's quite brilliant mind that God gave him, may not be exactly the same again. And there are still six treatments left. We obviously would not have made this choice if another one could be made, but somehow that knowledge did not mitigate the terrible heaviness I felt watching them put him in that machine.

And yet, we are here because God has a purpose for us. In cancer. In paralysis. In whole brain radiation. Certainly, there is sorrow in this place. At what life was before cancer. At still being whole while half of me is not.

But there is also hope. For God may yet restore all that has been lost and more. That, even if He does not, there is still a hope kept safe for us in heaven.

And here in the present, while God sees fit to have us in this place, we are upheld by His continual compassion, His unfailing mercy, and His never-ending steadfast love.

The day Matt *didn't* need to have a blood transfusion to live was a good day for me.

It meant that maybe, just maybe, the drug was working.

And maybe, just maybe, Matt would have a chance to recover from the stroke.

As his numbers finally came up, Matt started whole brain radiation.

Emotionally speaking, this was one of the hardest days for me of his entire hospital stay.

He was getting better in so many ways—his left hand was moving and his blood was stabilizing—and with everything in me, I did not want to do radiation on Matt because I loved his mind so much and knew that it would cause serious, long-term cognitive damage. But it was necessary to treat the tumors in his brain, and so, to radiation he went.

Walking down the hallway with him, I quoted Psalm 112:7 about how the righteous man is not afraid of bad news, both to him and to my own heart.

This was a hard moment, as was bringing the kids to see their daddy for the first time since he had his stroke.

When we told our kids about the cancer diagnosis, Matt and I were together. He led us through that as he had led us through everything else.

But when Matt had the stroke, I had to tell the kids on my own.

It never seemed like the right time to bring them in to see him, what with all the medical crises.

But one night, I realized that Matt had been in the hospital for over two weeks, and they had not seen him. And I realized that deep down, the real reason why I had not brought them in yet was because I was afraid.

I was afraid of how they might react, seeing Matt with no emotions and paralyzed. I was afraid of how Matt might react, of how I would manage it all.

When I realized that fear was the reason I hadn't brought them in, I resolved to bring them in the next day, to do the hard things and trust God with the outcome.

It was a hard meeting for our four little ones—aged 10, 9, 6, and 4—and it was brief. But my children got to see their daddy, got to tell him that they loved him, and he got to say it back.

With that first meeting, the worst was over.

The kids visited Matt about once a week from then on until he left the hospital and each time, it got a little bit easier, a little bit better.

Matt having no emotions was perhaps one of the hardest parts of that time. As he developed more and more movement on his left side, I would look for any indicators that emotions were coming back. An eyebrow lift. A tug at the corner of his mouth. But there seemed to be nothing and no promise there ever would be. It was a mountain I could not move, a dam I could not break.

But the Lord *is* compassionate.

He *is* merciful.

He doesn't give us more than we can bear.

And in His kindness, that dam was about to break.

CHAPTER 13

Weeping for Joy

February 25, 2017 *(Facebook Update)*

God's timing in all He does is perfect—never early and never late. I've thought about that a lot in the last few days as both the good and the challenging continue to make themselves known along this path.

First, the good: Matt is improving every day. In my last post, I said that the movement in his left hand was increasing and that another week I might be writing about his arm or his shoulder or his leg. In just one week's time, I am able to do just that. We have seen movement in his arm and shoulder and it continues to grow stronger each day. And yesterday, Matt was able to move the toes on his left foot for the first time since his stroke on February 2nd. This was huge! And such an answer to prayer!

As far as inside his body, his blood has only held steady and improved since my last post. These numbers tell us unequivocally that Matt is responding to the drug we were able to obtain—praise God for encouragements like these!

Now, for the other side of the coin.

Matt was officially approved for discharge from the hospital to rehab which was also good news...until he was rejected by the rehabilitation facility as a patient. He was rejected because our insurance has denied coverage for anything since Matt was admitted on February 2nd--the surgery, the radiation, the hospitalization--everything, and that includes rehabilitation. They are calling the cancer and everything resulting from it part of a pre-existing condition.

This is obviously problematic for us on multiple levels, one of which being that our hospital bill at this point is quite expensive. But by far the most immediate problem this presents for us is this: every day that goes by where Matt is just lying in a hospital bed, he is losing the muscle mass he still has on his right side. So, delaying his move into rehab is actually costly for us in terms of recovery.

The day I found out about this new turn of events, I submitted an appeal in what I hope was the best persuasive essay I've ever written. Since Wednesday, I've been on the phone with insurance companies, meeting with facilitators from the rehabilitation facility, and applying for other insurance coverage.

My week has been busy. And yet, I've thought much as I said about God's timing in all of this, about how He does not give us more than we can bear. I think if I had learned about this insurance thing when Matt was still in the ICU, when his life was hanging in the balance, it may have been too much for me to bear. But God's timing had this battle come to me now, when Matt is very much on the mend. And, though weary, I am up for the fight for a case I very much believe in.

We'll see what happens. But should our international insurance come back with another denial of my appeal, that decision, too, is in God's hands. As Proverbs informs us: "The king's heart is a stream of water in the hand of the Lord. He turns it wherever He wishes." God is sovereign over cancer, He's sovereign over strokes, and He is just as sovereign over insurance companies. That's where I rest and where I love to be.

The day Matt was approved for discharge from the hospital to rehab began as a day of rejoicing.

So many obstacles had been overcome in order for him to be stable enough to be released. Nearly everything that could have gone wrong in a lung cancer patient had gone wrong for him, and yet he had continued to battle through blood transfusions, fluid restrictions, whole-brain radiation, learning how to eat solid food again all just to get to this point.

We knew that for Matt to recover well, it was imperative he not lose any more muscle mass than he already had by spending over three weeks not moving in a hospital bed. He was ready, finally ready, to move on and learn how to walk again.

After the hospital approved him, I began packing our things when the hospital social worker told me rehab had denied him as a patient because Matt's international insurance had denied the claim.

They had not only denied this claim, but they had denied *all* of his claims since being admitted.

I was flummoxed. We were on an international insurance policy with IMG that should have covered this.

What I found out through a multitude of phone calls was that Matt's cancer was being labeled as a pre-existing condition based on a doctor's note that demonstrated it existed before we procured coverage—back in November of 2014, before we left for Papua New Guinea.

I knew this was impossible since Matt had had no symptoms before 2016.

When I returned home from the hospital that day, I spoke with the highest supervisor I could and asked every question I could think of—all to no avail. My only avenue was to submit an appeal and wait for up to *six weeks* for a response.

I hung up, completely discouraged.

To be denied coverage of *everything*—the last I checked, our hospital bills were in the neighborhood of $600,000—when we had paid for insurance was just unfathomable to me.

I was not anxious; I wasn't angry.

I was just weary.

Weary of almost losing Matt so many times.

Weary of balancing loving my husband at the hospital and loving my kids at home.

Weary of navigating the medical field.

And now, seeing on the horizon the necessity of navigating the insurance field, I was already weary of that, as well. These learning curves were so sharp, they could cut you in half.

I laid on my bedroom floor and just prayed, "Help."

Literally, I wasn't sure what to pray, except to just ask the Lord for help. I knew He would provide, one way or another.

But I also knew He would want me to do everything I could to fight.

So I got up, went to the couch, and, armed with every rhetorical device and fiber of my being, I wrote an appeal. And then I followed up on that appeal every other day, asking again for the basis of the findings and always hearing the same response, "We can't tell you anything. You'll know in six weeks."

I wished they could see Matt in that hospital bed, just for a moment, fighting so hard just to speak and move his left arm.

Six weeks? Did they have any idea the impact that time would have on his quality of life here in the time he had left?

Of all the bureaucratic challenges associated with Matt's cancer, this was the most difficult because I knew that the insurance company was wrong. And yet, they held such power over us in that moment.

But still, God is sovereign. Not even insurance companies can thwart His plan.

With hands empty of answers and running on fumes when it came to my strength, I went to the hospital the morning after writing the appeal.

At the time, my dad worked for the State of Arizona and suggested that I apply for AHCCCS, Arizona's Medicaid Agency. He gave me the name of a contact at the hospital who could help me apply.

I navigated my way through the hospital to the insurance office, tired but willing to fight this new fight. I wasn't alone as our pastor, Smedly, was again on hand to walk with me. We finished the application as quickly as we could and then headed back upstairs to Matt's room.

Because it was government insurance, I knew that it was unlikely for the process to move very fast.

But God is not limited by government processes.

I applied for AHCCCS on Thursday, and, my friends, I got a phone call on Monday telling me that Matt was approved. Not only were we approved, but the coverage would retroactively extend back to his date of diagnosis and cover *everything*.

It was provision beyond anything I could have thought possible.

To this day, I have not had to pay one penny of Matt's medical bills, a fact I still marvel at. I hear people complain sometimes about government and insurance, and I'm sure they have legitimate circumstances that warrant it, but all I can say is that our state insurance coverage has only ever been good to us.

As soon as the paperwork went through, Matt was moved to rehab.

I did eventually hear back from our insurance company about my appeal.

Long after Matt was making solid progress in rehab, they sent me an email explaining their decision. Their entire case was based on one note a doctor had written our first day at the hospital. She had written a date down for one of Matt's symptoms and gotten it wrong—*by a year*.

IMG denied us coverage based off of one doctor's incorrect date.

I reached out to an attorney friend of ours who works in insurance law. He sent them a letter, demanding they overturn their decision and cited multiple pieces of evidence. A month later, IMG responded back to the attorney as follows:

"After receiving your April 25, 2017 letter, we sent the matter for a second external peer review. The latest independent peer review physician concluded that your client's condition was not pre-existing…Thus, we overturned our decision."

They retroactively went back and paid for that which they should have paid at first.

*   *   *   *

When someone has a stroke and loses any amount of functionality, you always wonder, *will they ever get this back?*

Matt's emotions were near the top of my 'will-he-get-this-back' list.

I had watched as Matt's left hand had come back, and then his arm, and his leg. But his emotions were still absent.

And then, the morning of February 24th dawned, the day before the whole insurance fiasco began.

In college, Matt had made some very special, lifelong friends, each with their own awesome nickname: Swanny, Ruyle, Niner, and Hoost. They had been following Matt's illness and stroke and had asked if they might all be able to fly in together to see Matt.

So on February 24th, the four of them flew in from different parts of the world: Swanny from China, Ruyle from Washington D.C., Niner from Houston, and Hoost from San Diego.

Technically, Hoost might have driven—but regardless, they arrived at the hospital at the same time and made their way to Matt's room.

I'm not sure what I was expecting from this visit.

All I really knew was that Matt loved these guys, and these guys loved Matt. I was moved by the fact that these guys whom he hadn't seen in years were all willing to leave their families and fly—some from very far away!—to be with him.

I wasn't expecting much beyond a sweet visit, but what I got, and what Matt got, was much more.

These four big guys walked in through Matt's door, and the most amazing thing happened.

"Hi guys," Matt said.

And then, he began to cry.

"Matt," I said, staring at him. "You're crying!"

"I know!" he said.

And then everyone else in the room started crying.

It took four sweet friends coming thousands of miles and converging in one day, but in that moment, that mountain was moved, that dam broke, and God restored Matt's emotions.

The smile and the laughter would come later, but these tears—these precious tears we thought we might never see again—spun this moment of time into a strand of gold.

God did not have to give this back to us, but He did in such an extraordinary way—illustrating, once again, how much more extraordinary He is.

While those sweet friends were here, they were devoted to Matt, caring for him regardless of how uncomfortable the task might be. And when they were not with Matt, they were with me, fixing things at our house, cooking us dinner, taking my kids up on the roof of our house—because those are just the kind of unsafe shenanigans Matt would have pulled.

They came with us to church that Sunday, bravely sitting in our customary spot on the front row.

I'll never forget the sermon that day.

Our pastor had been working his way through Romans and the text was Romans 1:18-23 on the wrath of God.

Not necessarily what I would have chosen for first-time-visitors on the front row, but such an encouraging sermon!

It was like living water for my thirsty soul.

I was reminded, "That's right! Sin is still worse than cancer! Hell is still worse than any form of paralysis! Eternal destruction and separation from the one, true, good, living God is still far worse than radiation, brain tumors, and even death! And I will never experience that because Jesus died in my place 2,000 years ago!"

The timing of this sermon in the midst of having a paralyzed, terminally ill husband and no insurance was such a gift. Because as bad as my bad news was, there was something much worse. And Matt and I had already been rescued from it!

It's hard to express just how well the Lord sustained me during these weeks. Given what an anxious, fearful person I am by nature, He kept me from so much anxiety and fear.

In the days and weeks that followed, the rest of Matt's emotions came back. His facial expressions, his smile, the inflection in his voice, God restored it all to him within another month.

Needless to say, the day I got to take a picture with my husband (somewhat) smiling again is near the top of the list for the one for which I will always be most grateful!

MARCH-APRIL

CHAPTER 14

I've Got the Lord

March 5, 2017 (*Facebook Update*)

By God's grace and kindness, Matt is now in rehab.

In a whirlwind of insurance changes, he was accepted as a patient into the rehabilitation facility and approved by our new insurance on Thursday.

There are so many wonderful things about being in rehab. Like the fact Matt is stable enough to be there. And how the staff doesn't treat Matt like something frail that needs to be coaxed back into life. In the hospital, the goal was to get Matt stable and healed enough to leave. In rehab, the goal is to work Matt as hard as he's able in order for him to stand and perhaps one day walk again.

Matt has to learn to do everything all over again--from eating and drinking, to sitting, standing, bathing, etc. all while starting with no movement at all in his left leg and a very weak left upper body. Cognitively, the part of the brain where Matt's bleed occurred affects much of how he operates—planning, memory, problem solving, concentration—and will need to be rehabilitated as well.

We are having to learn patience in a way we have never had to before. It is the kind of patience where you wait to see whether things may or may not come back tomorrow; where things that once were as easy as breathing are now very, very hard; where sometimes you wake up at two in the morning and can do nothing but wait until morning, unable to do little but pray. And all of that occurs before you remember that there is still stage IV lung cancer to fight.

It's encouraging, then, that our example for patience comes from God, whose patience is infinite. He was patient with us every day before we were saved, enduring our indifference, our rejection, our rebellion towards Him. He is patient with us still as we stumble and repent and rise again by His grace. And today He is patient with a world that so often does not deign to acknowledge Him—yet all the while still offers eternal life through Jesus Christ His Son to all who would believe!

The other day, while still in the hospital, I asked Matt's oncologist about reasons for his fatigue and he responded for me to take my pick.

"Side effects of the drugs he's taking, side effects from radiation. Trauma to the brain from the stroke, trauma to the brain from the surgery after the stroke—he's got about twelve different reasons to be fatigued. Plus, he's probably a little depressed."

From the hospital bed, Matt shook his head emphatically.

"You're not depressed?" the oncologist asked.

Matt shook his head again and then replied slowly, "I'm happy."

"Why are you happy?" asked the doctor.

There was a pause as Matt formulated his thoughts and then said, "Because I've got the Lord."

"Well, I don't understand that," the oncologist shook his head. "Because if I was lying in that bed, I would be depressed."

These things, these trials, these kinds of sufferings, Romans 5 tells us, are producing endurance which in turn produces character. And character, dear friends, produces hope. And this hope will never disappoint us, it will never put us to shame, because it is founded and grounded in Jesus, who also endured and persevered, that we might do the same for the glory of God in whatever circumstances He gives us—be they traversing mountains in a village in Papua New Guinea or lying in a hospital bed with cancer in Phoenix, Arizona.

So we are not depressed.

And we are not overwhelmed.

We remember our hope and lift up our heads and keep waiting, keep enduring, keep our eyes fixed on the One who ran this race long before us, because in Him is all our hope and strength and joy, both for this present moment and for all of eternity.

The remarkable thing about Matt was that he was the same in his lowest moments that he was at his highest.

When I asked the oncologist about his fatigue and he offered depression as a possible reason, it took everything within me to keep my mouth shut.

Our whole marriage, I had always been too quick to speak, whereas Matt tried to actually think before he spoke. When someone would ask us something, I would have to exercise a lot of self-control to not answer first all the time. Often, I would try to just look at Matt and wait for him to answer, counting to ten in my mind, Mississippis and all.

The moment the oncologist mentioned depression, even though I knew Matt was paralyzed and sick, and possibly asleep, I did the same thing.

I shut my mouth and waited because, with everything in me, I wanted to deny that Matt was depressed, that his hope was not in his body or his circumstances, that even sleeping that man had the joy of the Lord.

But I couldn't do that because, one, the question was not mine to answer, and two, I wasn't one hundred percent sure he wasn't depressed. He had been sleeping so much and interacting so little.

Was he depressed?

I looked at Matt whose eyes were still closed and waited.

One Mississippi, two Mississippi...

And then he gave an answer far better than any I could have given.

The oncologist seemed taken aback by his answer. Matt's response, I imagine, was probably unusual amongst all the cancer patients he must see each day.

There was Matt, weak, paralyzed, still dying of cancer, telling this man that he was happy, even in the midst of all those things because he had the Lord.

Had he not been paralyzed, he would have said the same thing, albeit with a bit more inflection and perhaps with his eyes open.

The oncologist left shortly after the exchange—he never stayed long—but standing there, I thought how Matt in his suffering might have just accomplished more for the Lord in two sentences with this man than someone with full health and more eloquent words could have.

*   *   *   *

Rehab was a struggle.

Matt, still fatigued from radiation, had to suddenly adapt to an environment that expected much more from him than having stable sodium levels.

The great part about rehab is that they set aggressive goals for you in order to gain back what you've lost. But in order to set goals for him, the therapists first had to assess how much he had actually lost.

Some of what Matt had lost was obvious.

Physically, he had lost a solid forty pounds—a substantial amount of weight for his already lean frame.

Mentally, he had lost some cognitive alacrity, and his appointment with his speech therapist and counting games was slightly discouraging.

The only solution for getting better was to work hard, and that is exactly what Matt did.

When he first got to rehab, Matt could move his left arm—not too high or too quickly, but he could move it. Every day he worked hard at his exercises to strengthen it. The sheer effort it took for him to pick up a small ring and drop it around the neck of a small wooden pole was painful to watch. But he kept at it and made progress, bit by bit.

His leg, we weren't sure about. So far, we had seen some on-command toe-wiggling, but that was about it.

Still, Matt was thrilled with his progress in his left hand because with it, he could type and text again!.

The day after this post, Matt texted me:

Matt: "I texted Jake this morning. It was so awesome."

Me: "Oh, praise the Lord for texting, huh?"

Matt: "I also moved my left leg a little this morning!!"

Me: "What?! What do you mean?"

Matt: "I'll show you later.☺ I mean, I just moved it a little, but still."

Me: "Hello! Just moving it a little is all your hand started with…and then your arm…and then your shoulder! I'm just going to pray that you can start walking next week. ☺"

The laughter, too, came back.

One day, we were in Matt's rehab room watching a Planet Earth episode about how snow leopards mark their territories with their scent. I made some sort of a joke about how I would mark Matt's territory with my scent—something totally normal like that—and Matt made a sound.

I wasn't sure what it was, but the next day, I told the joke again with my mom there and Matt made the same sound.

Was that sound…laughter?

The joke was certainly funny enough to warrant it.

Any doubts disappeared the following day as I was laughing about how everyone was saying what an inspirational couple we were. My mom joked that we should hang a plaque above our bed with the words 'Inspirational Couple' written on it, to which I added that we would then have a picture of Matt and me and our golden retriever, Bodhi.

At this, Matt laughed for real.

God only knows why this was so funny to him, but he laughed every time I repeated this joke for the next two days. It was the sweetest sound I had heard in a long time.

Sometimes, God flies four of your closest friends from all different parts of the world to restore your emotions.

And sometimes, He just uses the ridiculously funny wife right next to you.

March 13, 2017 *(Facebook Update)*

It's been 60 days since Matt's diagnosis and 39 since his stroke. Many of those days have been filled with bad news and uncertainty.

But in God's goodness, today was not one of those days.

Today, I got to see my husband walk again.

Not on his own—he had to use a walker. And not without a physical therapist walking very closely behind him.

But he walked.

Over the course of just a week and a half in rehab, Matt has regained the use of his left side almost completely. It is still very weak and not always consistent. And the challenges to get Matt to where he used to be are significant and far from guaranteed. But after seeing Matt's progress today, the physical therapist cancelled the wheelchair she had been planning to send home with us.

Even with this improvement, however, things are not all sunshine and roses. At the end of the day, Matt still has Stage IV lung cancer.

We are still living with a sentence of death. Indeed, we are not promised tomorrow--none of us are! But, oh! How thankful we are for today!

Still, we know that had God not given Matt back any of this, He would have done us no wrong. He has already given us life and breath and almost 12 years with each other. He has given us food to eat every day and clothes to wear and our four beautiful kids! But more than any of those things is that which He has given us which we consider most precious of all—salvation from our sin through His Son!

God's steadfast love towards us was not proved today when Matt walked again, but 2,000 years ago when Jesus took our place on that cross and purchased on our behalf freedom from our sin and an eternity with Him.

There is so much brokenness in this world, so much sin, so many burdens carried. I marvel at how this one hope outweighs all of them. How the light that came into this world is so bright, that all who look to Him to be saved will never see complete darkness again. How that future weight of glory awaiting us in heaven will ultimately make this ravaging of Matt's body and blood look light and momentary.

It was once our plan to declare this hope in the remote mountains of Papua New Guinea. But now, we will declare it here. Or wherever we are. Declare hope to the hopeless, light in the darkness, and the truth of the One who carries the burdens we cannot, who carried them completely on the cross.

So tonight, as Matt and I fall asleep, still in separate places and still with a terminal illness in our lives, we rejoice in that truth that will never change, both on the days of bad news which have come and will likely come again, and on days like today, with very, very good news.

"Okay," the physical therapist said, as she helped Matt get to a walker. "Now, go ahead and walk."

"Walk?" Matt asked in disbelief.

"Yes," she replied, smiling.

We were all shocked at the command. Since gaining it back, Matt hadn't done much activity with his left leg.

But he looked at me, looked at the physical therapist, and then he walked.

It was a little bit more of a shuffle, and she kept her hand on the safety belt around his waist the whole time, but the man walked down the hallway on his own.

Writing this book is hard sometimes because I know how this story ends.

But when I reflect back on this time, yes, there are some drops of bitter. But, my friends, for every drop of bitter the Lord gave us, there was a whole cupful of sweet.

God's goodness to us the day Matt walked again is not negated by the fact that he would not walk for much longer.

It was a sweet moment of victory that would have been cherished by all of us, regardless of how long he lived. We are still inestimably grateful for it.

As Matt's left side got stronger, he was able to return to reading his Bible and his Greek New Testament.

He was also able to write out his prayers again. Just a few days before he would walk, he wrote out a prayer for the first time since his stroke on February 2nd.

3/10/2017

"God, I'm in rehab and I need your help. Please give me energy for today. Please help me to excel in physical therapy. Please may I be able to walk again! Please God, restore my leg and arm. May I try so hard today! God, thank you for being able to read the Bible. Thank You for rehab. God, again, please may we trust You and may we be content in whatever You send our way. God, please really if You could restore me completely that would be awesome, but whatever Your will is, God! By life or death, may You be glorified in my body!"

With every week that went by, Matt sounded more and more like himself:

3/17/2017

"God, it's Friday night, and I'm still in rehab, but wanted to just say thank You for answering my prayers! Thank You for more progress today! Please may it continue everyday through the rest of my time in rehab! Please, God, may I work hard, push myself, and remember to use my left side. Please restore my mind, my leg, my arm, everything, just like Nebuchadnezzar, and please may I not be like that king who forgot all the good You did for him! Please help Cameron to shepherd her heart, and please sustain our kids through all of this! Please kill the cancer, too (I always forget about that part)."

In our text messages, he would sometimes refer to his left hand in the third person because, even though he could move it now, it still didn't quite feel like a part of him.

Matt: "I feel so good today! I brushed my teeth standing up. My left hand is doing so much better at typing today, too! I'm so proud of the little guy. I'm thinking about making him an official left hand again if he keeps up the good work."

As he continued to make progress, he got to go on the occasional field trip with one of his therapists.

Sends me a picture of him smiling with one of his nurses pushing his wheelchair)
Matt: "Heading to Starbucks. One of the nurses took me—it was fun. He took this back way in and I was like, shoot, we have not explored this hospital enough! We should know about this back way by now!"

Matt getting his sense of humor back was like a runner getting his legs back.

By God's grace, he had made it through a terminal diagnosis, a life-threatening stroke, paralysis and he was still the exact same guy!

A little slower, maybe.

But that just gave me the advantage I had been waiting for to finally be the funniest one in our marriage.

Matt quickly became a favorite in rehab.

He thanked everybody, even if the exercise was hard. He was always joyful, even when there were days of discouragement or slow progress. And he was always pointing to God as the source of that joy.

Once, his physical therapist asked him about why he was so positive all the time.

"Well, I think a lot of it is my personality, just how I'm made," Matt replied. "But it's also because I know the Lord!"

CHAPTER 15

God is Still Good!

March 20, 2017 (*Facebook Update*)

Last week, I asked Matt to write down some of the thoughts he has had since the stroke. I expected a few sentences because writing is still not the easiest task for him. He surpassed my expectations as he has done this whole time.

Here is what he wrote:

"It's March 15th and I have about two weeks of rehab left. I've been in the hospital now for about six weeks, but the first four were the most difficult weeks of my life, and I don't actually remember all of it.

"There was one day this past week where I was telling Cameron a hard story from when I was in the ICU and then she told me a hard story from when I was in the ICU, and I'm just like, that's awful! How did you do that? I was not aware my life was on the line. So, after talking to Cameron and her mom, I've determined that their hard times were much harder than my hard times....at least in a different way.

"When I was still in the ICU and the hospital, there were many times where I would just be in the midst of a very difficult situation and I'd stop and think back at what I said that Sunday before the stroke, and just ask myself, do I still believe God is good?

"Every time the answer was a resounding 'Yes!' At times, it almost felt like the trials came in waves, each one beating against me, and asking me, "Is God still good?!" and after coming out of the wave, I would just muster my energy and yell, "Yes, God is still good!"

"Look, it has been a huge trial, but I'm still not getting what I deserve! I still know the one true God and will be with Him for all eternity (and oh, how I long for that day!). God has done me no wrong in bringing me low. I think Job's incorrect thinking was that he thought bad things only happen to bad people, and Job was indeed a righteous man, so bad things shouldn't have been happening to him.

"But as we have said before, there are no good people. I mean, I've been declared righteous and have Christ's righteousness, but I've never done anything to deserve a cancer-free life or even a hell-free life! I've sinned against the perfect and holy God who created the heavens and the earth, and I deserve wrath which would be an eternity in hell, and I'm still alive—more than that, I know God and have been forgiven all my sins! I have still only received grace upon grace!

"What's crazy now, is that four weeks ago, I had lost so much—the ability to eat, sleep, walk, drink, have a bowel movement of any kind, talk, laugh, cry, smile, read, think clearly, speak clearly, type, use my arm. Four weeks ago, I had a feeding tube, an oxygen mask, and a PICC line through which I was getting transfusions every 24 hours. I remember just lying in the hospital bed during those days and talking to God and just being like, 'God, You have brought me low.'

"In these last weeks, though, we have also seen so many mercies of God. I can now eat again and smile and laugh and cry and drink. I'm walking with a walker and having conversations and moving my arm and typing and reading and am still alive! I don't deserve any of these things, and yet God has seen fit to give them back. Praise God! His mercies are new every morning, and I literally see that here every morning! Even more, I have felt and seen so much love from so many people! I mean, the love from the body of Christ has been amazing and just a huge kindness and blessing from God.

"How God has sustained my wife through all of this is amazing, and just how much grace I see in her as she has had to weather all of this is just such a kindness of God. She has never once said, "Just curse God and die", but has been steadfast, immovable, and such an encouragement to me. We have seen so many answers to prayer here and so many other things, it would be difficult to write them all.

"I pray prayers that I think some may think are silly. I pray, 'God, please restore me back to health' and, 'God, please take the cancer away'. And, yes, I do believe that the God who healed blind men, and paraplegics, and bleeding disorders, and raised the dead can heal me!

And at the same time, whatever the Lord wills for me, I will, by God's grace, be content with.

"So, I write this because I almost felt the need to just tell the world, "Hey, we are still holding to what we said, by God's grace! God is still good! I still know my Savior! I have not and will not waver from what we originally said! God has just actually been kind and merciful in all of this! We are still not getting what we deserve. These light momentary afflictions are still not even close to being compared to the glory that will be revealed to us."

Sometime after this post, someone handed me a gift bag, and inside was a custom-made sign that read, "'YES! God is still good'—Matt Dodd". That was the banner flying over Matt's life in times of health, and, by God's grace, cancer and stroke did not change it.

Though Matt was walking with a walker, he longed to be back to normal:

3/20/2017

"God, it's Monday morning! Another day of therapy, and I feel like I slept pretty well last night! God, please give me energy today to work hard. Please may walking not be an idol. It is hard, God, I do desperately want to walk again. Please help my heart not put my hope in walking, but in You! And please restore me back to my original self! It would be sweet if at the end of this, I'm walking again, and the cancer is gone! May I be bold with the gospel, God! I mean, if anything, I should learn from this that life is short. Every person I meet could enter into eternity at any time."

Sooner than I could have hoped, we were scheduling Matt for discharge. He wrote:

3/21/2017

"God, it's Tuesday. I get out of rehab in one week! I'm so excited...and nervous, God! God, I beg you to restore me! Please may I be able to play with my kids again, and be able to help around the house, and, God, please may I just

be restored back to health! Please be gracious, God...please may I be sanctified and grow through all of this!

"God, thank You for how You are using this trial to encourage others. Please may I go through this trial in a way worthy of You! Please, God, may I give you all the glory. Please continue to heal me and restore me back to health! God, please may I not be like Hezekiah or one of the other kings that forgot about you after you worked a miracle, and please, God, continue to help me make progress! May I be able to get stronger and stronger every day! God, please may I be able to walk and be restored! Even now, God, as I get ready to go to physical therapy, please give me energy to work hard! Please use us, God, when we speak to the body as well!"

While he was still in rehab, I continued to bring the kids in once a week for a family movie night with Daddy.

When I first brought them in, Matt couldn't make it through the whole movie because sitting in the wheelchair for that long was too uncomfortable for him. But by the time our last family movie night there rolled around, he was not only making it to the end of movies, he was enjoying them! Seeing the kids talk to their Dad the way they used to was yet one more thing the Lord had restored.

Before discharge, Matt had a whole new set of scans.

Every scan showed the same thing: a dramatic reduction of the cancer in his body and his brain. The medicine was working even better than we had hoped.

Our pastors had again asked Matt if he would like to say something to our church body when he got out of rehab, and he had again said yes.

Preparing what he would say proved much more challenging than the last time, however, as organizing his thoughts and writing them down took more time.

During his rounds with his physical therapist, occupational therapist, and speech therapist that last week in rehab, he would excitedly tell everyone what he was speaking on.

"It's called "Four Truths to Sustain a Dying Man," he would say. He would tell them the outline and then invite them to come hear him the following Sunday.

When the Sunday came for him to speak, almost every therapist and oncologist with whom he had interacted was sitting in that room.

In the days leading up the speaking, Matt prayed about speaking and the uncertainty of his circumstances:

3/26/2017

"God, please help me today! I feel like every day is a little fragile and unknown. I don't know if I have brain tumors or cancer growing, I don't know if today is going to be my last, or if I'm going to live for a long time! So, God, please may I not cling to this world, may I not assume that everything is always going to be fine, but please, God, may I just trust in You each day, and ask You for help each day, not expecting or needing anything, but being content with whatever You have for me.

"God, I do ask though that You would continue to make me better. Please make me new again, and please may You heal me from this cancer. God, thank You for giving me my arm back and bringing back my leg. God, I pray I would be diligent at home to work hard, exercise, and that You would show me favor and continue to heal me.

"God, please give me words to say to encourage the body on Sunday, and please give me the strength to say it! God, prepare me for discharge tomorrow. Please help my transition into normal life go well. Please help me to love my wife, and still be a help at home. God, please give us wisdom basically to navigate these waters to Your glory. I do pray, God, that You could use me to preach the gospel to people and encourage the body. I think You already have used this, but please continue to use us, like this Sunday, God. Please may I speak clearly, and may my content be clear and encouraging! Please help Cameron today to be encouraged and make it through the day. God, please help us, and also please help me to be able to pray for others more, and not be so focused on myself!"

The day of his discharge, Matt thanked God for bringing him so far.

3/27/2017

"God, it's Monday morning, the day of discharge from rehab, and it's early. I'm so excited to go home, and so thankful for Your kindness in all of this. I feel kind of dumb for ever having a little doubt that You could do the things I was asking You to do, because You have done everything so far and been so gracious. God, please restore me completely, and please guard my heart from pride and hoping in this world and forgetting about Your kindness to me! God, please give Cameron and I strength today to make it through this day. Please give me strength and endurance and wisdom in the coming days to be able to be at home, love my wife, love my kids, and just move and live again! God, I do pray that my cognitive abilities would remain intact for years to come and there would be no long-term side effects from the brain radiation."

On March 27th, Matt walked out to our minivan with his walker, and, after 53 days in the hospital, my husband was at home with his family.

The next few days were spent adjusting to life with Matt home.

3/28/2017

"God, it's my first morning back at home, and I'm getting ready to read Your word! God, thank You for bringing me back! Thank You for my wife and her help. Thank You for this house, God, and for how You have provided for us so well! God, please help me today to have energy and to be able to walk better, and talk better, and do everything better at home. God, please may I be able to do this! Please, as I have prayed, restore me back to my original self! Please may I walk and run and ride a bike and climb and drive!

"Please give me words to say at church, God, may I be encouraging. God, please continue to shrink the cancer, keep us humble and relying upon You. I mean, I can die at any time! God, please help me to trust You in this and live my life for Your glory and not be ashamed of the Gospel. Please help me now as I read Your Word to be encouraged."

We had a "Welcome Home, Matt" party where about a hundred people dropped by. Every time I would glance at Matt, he would be smiling and laughing with someone new, catching my eye and taking steps without his walker just to show me what a daredevil he was.

After the party, Matt focused on what he was planning to say that Sunday at church:

3/29/2017

"God, once again, I just come to You begging for help. I'm home from the hospital, it's day three, and it's been such a good day, God! God thank You for the stroke, thank You that I have this opportunity to give You glory! Really, I mean, the path here, I would never like to walk again, but at the same time, I'm thankful for being thankful for everything—for seeing You uphold my faith, for seeing the love of the body of Christ, for my family and friends, and for salvation, God! You truly are such a good God! Thank You for choosing me, and loving me, and caring for me!

"God, please use me Sunday to speak to Your church. Please may I speak from my heart, and encourage the body, and please give me words to say. God, please may I not boast in my own ability, but in You alone!"

CHAPTER 16

Four Truths to Sustain a Dying Man

April 2, 2017 (*Matt speaks to the body of Grace Bible Church for the first time since the stroke*)

Hello everyone! It is so good to be back.

The last several weeks have been the hardest weeks of our lives and God has sustained us through it all. Right now, I'm not going to preach a sermon. I'm going to give a testimony of God's grace in our lives.

But my testimony has a title and it has four points. The title is "Four Truths to Sustain a Dying Man."

The first truth that sustains me, the dying man, is that <u>we have a hope in heaven</u>.

Philippians 3:20-21 says, "But our citizenship is in heaven, and from it we await a Savior, the Lord Jesus Christ, who will transform our lowly body to be like his glorious body, by the power that enables him even to subject all things to himself."

When I was in the ICU, I was in bad shape. I couldn't speak. I couldn't laugh. I had no emotions and my whole left side was paralyzed. I lay in that bed and couldn't move. It was so hard, so uncomfortable laying in a bed for hours and hours without being able to adjust yourself.

And yet, as I lay there during that time, at the bottom of the worst part of this, I thought about that verse. I thought, "I have a citizenship in heaven!" It sustained me knowing that I have a hope in heaven. And it is so secure. We have an inheritance that is imperishable, undefiled, unfading. It's not something that is *being* prepared for us—it's there!

We have it right now! And it's described in God's Word as something so much better than this life. This life is so good. We have friends and family and beautiful things. Yet, God didn't save us to have a better life here. He saved us so that we can see Him face to face one day!

2 Corinthians 5:1-2 says, "For we know that if the tent that is our earthly home is destroyed, we have a building from God, a house not made with hands, eternal in the heavens. For in this tent we groan, longing to put on our heavenly dwelling…"

While I lay in that bed, I was groaning; my earthly tent was being destroyed. I longed to put on my heavenly dwelling.

I tried to contemplate what heaven will be like during that time. I tried to come up with analogies to compare it to, but my analogies never fully worked.

You can go to the Grand Canyon and be moved by the largeness of it and the beauty of it. You can see a thunderstorm and be awed by its power and get goosebumps from the wind and the rain. You can try to comprehend space and be flabbergasted by the immensity and complexity of it. Yet, God is more amazing than the Grand Canyon. He's more awe-inspiring than a thunderstorm. He is more incomprehensible than space. This is the God who saved us to Himself!

I can truly agree with the Apostle Paul throughout all of this, "For to me to live is Christ, and to die is gain" (Philippians 1:21).

This sure hope in heaven, of being with our glorious God, sustained me, the dying man, throughout this trial and continues to do so today.

The second truth that sustains this dying man is that <u>I will never suffer as much as my Savior suffered for me.</u>

In order to understand this point, you have to first understand one more statement: I am not getting what I deserve.

Twelve weeks ago, we stood up here and we said, God is just and good in giving us this cancer.

Why? Because we don't deserve anything good in this life. We have sinned against a holy God and we deserve wrath, eternal punishment from Him. We are not "good". There are no "good" people in this world. We don't deserve anything good. All my sins against this holy and "good" Creator earned me an eternal punishment. My rebellion against Him was and is deserving of eternal death, but God, in His kindness and mercy, has actually given me eternal life!

How has He accomplished this? This is what brings us to this statement: I will never suffer as much as my Savior suffered for me, because He bore my wrath. Jesus took that eternal punishment my sins deserved when He died on the cross. I am not getting what I do deserve, because Jesus took what He didn't deserve! He didn't deserve to be mistreated or beaten or spit upon or crucified or bear my sin and punishment. But He did it for me! He did it for every believer.

Mark 10:45 says, "For even the Son of Man came not to be served but to serve, and to give his life as a ransom for many."

When I was in the ICU, I was uncomfortable almost to the point of anguish. It's hard to even describe. It was the worst time in my life, and yet, my God was pierced for my transgressions. He was crushed for my sin. He was nailed to a cross, but even more, He bore all the wrath that I deserved. Jesus suffered on the cross far more than I could ever suffer in this life.

Even now as I think about the future, there are so many bad things that could happen.

My doctor is here.

I could ask him, "What are all the bad things that could happen, Dr. Polowy?"

I still have cancer. It could keep growing or grow back. It's shrinking now, praise God, but I got full brain radiation. That doesn't sound good, right? The side effects from that, I'm praying that God minimizes, that I just forget things I don't really need to know like facts about donkeys and cows and stuff. There are all these plausible situations that could occur in the future, but I know that I will **NEVER** suffer in any of these situations as much as my Savior suffered for me to save me.

2 Corinthians 5:21 says, "For our sake he made him to be sin who knew no sin, so that in him we might become the righteousness of God."

This truth that I will never suffer as much as Christ suffered for me and that I will never get what I do deserve because Jesus got what he didn't deserve has sustained me, the dying man, during this time.

The third truth that sustains this dying man is that <u>Christians love one another</u>.

John 13:35 says, "By this, all people will know that you are my disciples, if you have love for one another." Seeing the love of my brothers and sisters in Christ has brought me to tears on multiple occasions.

I didn't have emotions for the longest time and four of my friends flew out just to see me. When I saw them, it was the first time that I started crying again after having the stroke. It was amazing! It moved me to tears, just the love that our brothers and sisters showed us.

1 Corinthians 1:25-26 says, "...that there may be no division in the body, but that the members may have the same care for one another. If one member suffers, all suffer together; if one member is honored, all rejoice together."

I never felt like we were alone in any of this.

I mean, I don't think I was alone for a day in the hospital or anywhere the whole time. I did feel and experience that when one member suffers, all suffer together. Thank you, guys, for suffering with us! It is God's love displayed through the body of Christ that sustained us during this time.

But I want to list one person, in particular, that needs to be recognized.

I'll give some Scripture to give it away: "Charm is deceitful, and beauty is vain, but a woman who fears the Lord is to be praised" (Proverbs 31:30).

I didn't practice this part with Cameron, so she has no idea what I'm going to say. My wife has been a rock during all of this. She has feared Yahweh and has not feared her husband dying.

(*Looking at Cameron*) Maybe you were a little afraid, but for the most part you feared Yahweh. God has shown her much grace and sustained her so well. She has had to watch her husband come near to death on multiple occasions, being a solo mom for two months and needing to navigate insurance and finances and communication…I mean, my wife is amazing!

Proverbs 31:10-12 says, "An excellent wife who can find? She is far more precious than jewels. The heart of her husband trusts in her, and he will have no lack of gain. She does him good, and not harm, all the days of her life."

An excellent wife who can find?

(*Points at Cameron enthusiastically*) I found her!! She's right here! She is sitting next to me and she has been next to me this entire time. God has sustained me, the dying man, by the love that Christians show to one another.

The last truth that sustained this dying man is that <u>God loves us.</u>

Ephesians 3:18-19 says, "(so that you) may have strength to comprehend with all the saints what is the breadth and length and height and depth, and to know the love of Christ that surpasses knowledge, that you may be filled with all the fullness of God."

It would have been enough to be justified, to be adopted, to be able to go to heaven, but God loves us! I think about all the people who have shown us love during this time and it was so great to be loved, and yet, God's love is so much greater! It is incomprehensible.

At the end of the day, God hasn't proven His love for us because I'm standing here now or because the cancer is shrinking.

His love was proven at the cross. God loved us and sent His Son to die for sinners. That's the kind of love that God displays. It's amazing! And this love is steadfast. It doesn't change. It's not like I've gotten cancer because God hates me. It's still this love that God displayed at the cross that is behind every act in my life, everything that comes into my life. And it's this love that I will try to comprehend for all eternity.

The fourth truth that sustained me, the dying man, is that God loves me and loves us!

189

These last couple months were, again—this is my conclusion—the most difficult times of my life. God so graciously sustained us with these truths.

But really, we are all dying men and women, right?

I am going to have to die someday. We are all going to have to die someday. If you are here and you do not have a hope, if you are not sure where you are going to go when you die, know that God offers forgiveness for your sins. You can be saved right now by trusting in Jesus Christ. But in order to be saved you have to recognize that you need saving. You have to recognize that you are a sinner. That you have sinned against this God, and the only way to be right before Him is to trust in the salvation that He's provided in Jesus Christ. You can have a hope in heaven right now by trusting in Jesus Christ!

Romans 10:9 says, "...if you confess with your mouth that Jesus is Lord and believe in your heart that God raised him from the dead, you will be saved."

And Ephesians 2:8-9 says, "For by grace you have been saved through faith. And this is not your own doing; it is the gift of God, not a result of works, so that no one may boast."

It is very clear from Scripture that salvation is not by works, not by any good thing that we could try to do or by being good people, but through faith alone in the Son of God, Jesus Christ, alone.

Our biggest prayer in all of this is: "...it is my eager expectation and hope that I will not be at all ashamed, but that with full courage now as always Christ will be honored in my body, whether by life or by death. For to me to live is Christ, and to die is gain" (Philippians 1:20-21). That really is our prayer in all of this; that God would be honored in my body, whether by life or by death.

Because who knows?

We still don't know what is going to happen. We are praying for life, but God could take me tomorrow or the next day. We are just praying that God would be honored by my life or my death.

There have been times in this where I thought, "Should I freak out about this? Should I become discouraged or scared or anxious? Cameron and I both had this conversation where we had this thought,

"We should probably be freaking out more". Or be depressed or something.

But my response was, "How could I?!" We have a hope in heaven! I will never suffer as much as my Savior suffered for me! I have brothers and sisters who love me. I know the living God who loves me!

"Who has spoken and it came to pass, unless the Lord has commanded it? Is it not from the mouth of the Most High that good and bad come? Why should a living man complain, a man, about the punishment of his sins?" (Lamentations 3:37-39).

I feel like responding with depression would be denying these truths. It would be like saying, "I don't have a wife or kids." But that's not true. I love my wife and kids!

Regardless of the circumstances on any given day, we are blessed beyond measure. Cameron and I kept saying throughout all of this: "This is the day that the LORD has made; let us rejoice and be glad in it" (Psalm 118:24).

And every day that we said that it was true. Every day is the day that the Lord has made, and there is so much to rejoice and be glad in.

Do I have cancer? Yes.

Could I die? Sure.

Could it go really bad? Maybe.

But, do I know the one true living God? YES! Do I have a hope in heaven? YES! Will I ever suffer in this world as much as my Savior suffered for me on the cross? No, I won't! Do I have brothers and sisters in Christ who love us? Yes, I do. Does God love me more than I could ever comprehend? Yes!

So, this is the day that the Lord has made. We can rejoice and be glad in it!"

April 2, 2017

"God, it's Sunday night and You were once again gracious in answering our prayers today. Thank You for using us in this way. I pray, God, for even more fruitful labor; that You would heal me from this cancer, make me strong again, make me run again, and please give us fruitful ministry! God, I do pray that many would hear the gospel and repent and believe. God, please use us to be bold and unashamed of the gospel here in this neighborhood and in this world!"

With Matt home, the battles before us suddenly became much smaller.

We went to the gym on most days. Matt was excited about working out and getting his strength back. The first time we went to the gym, we left the walker in the car, as I was confident we could do it with him holding my hand.

We never used it again.

Occasionally, there were small scares.

Like the time Matt's bilirubin levels were high in his liver which threatened his use of Alectinib, since a possible side effect of the drug was damage to the liver.

In response to this threat, Matt prayed the following:

4/4/2017

"God, it's Thursday morning, and I found out yesterday that my bilirubin levels are high. God, please may this not be a result of the Alectinib. God, please may I continue on this drug, because it seems like it's working so well. But maybe You have something else in store for me. God, please may we trust You, and once again, if I have to stop taking this medicine, and the cancer starts winning again, that would just be Your will, and we can trust You with that. God, I do ask that You heal me somehow though, that You would use us here on this earth, that our kids would have a dad, that my wife would have a husband, and that I would be around and that You could still use me to make Your gospel known.

"Please make me bold God with Your gospel. I feel like I've maybe settled into an easy life after being back from the hospital. Please remind me that life is short, and please fill me with boldness and a hope in You!"

And then there was the pain.

It was confusing because sometimes Matt's back hurt as a result from being inactive for so long in the hospital.

Sometimes, his stomach hurt because of constipation. It was hard to always nail down exactly why something was hurting. But overall, Matt's body was getting stronger, and his pain was decreasing.

As a family, we ate together, laughed together, went to church together, and watched our favorite TV shows together.

Matt was a bit slower to get the jokes and sometimes would miss them altogether, which was a stab to my heart occasionally, but as far as stroke recovery went, progress was being made every day.

We also talked about the future.

Now that it seemed Matt was on the mend, we would have to plan out a different future than the one we were planning on in Papua New Guinea.

Matt prayed:

4/6/2017

"God, it's so good to be back home! And You are still making me stronger and stronger every day. God, please continue to use us in all of this.

"We don't know what we are going to be doing moving forward. I'll be rehabilitating. But I can't do that all day. Technically I can, but I need to have a job to do at some point. God, please provide a job. God, You have been so gracious and kind throughout all this. Please, God, make me one of those outlier cases where I am cured from the cancer! Please may I be able to hike again, and camp again, and surf again, and run again, and rock climb again.

"And yet at the same time, whatever You will, may we just be content, God. Please provide the grace that we need to be able to be content in whatever situation. God, we praise You for restoring me already so much. I don't deserve any of these good things.

"Please may we grow so close to You during this time and honor You! God, please reveal what You want us to do as well....write a book? Go back to school? Engineering? Pastoring? God, please provide some means at some point for us to have work! God, You are good, and really I'm glad to be back, but this really is nothing compared to being in Your presence! And I'm going to need to come there some day. Give me a content heart, God, and help me to be patient and kind today."

It was a struggle for Matt to reclaim his former routine in the weeks after he came home, but his desire was always to be in the word of God.

Cancer or no cancer, stroke or no stroke, Matt knew that his time with the Lord in the morning was the most important thing, and he fought for it:

4/11/2017

"God, it's Tuesday morning and I slept in! I slept in! God, I can't be sleeping in like this. Please help me to wake up early. Please instill a dependence upon You in all of this. Thank You for this time right now, to sit here and talk to You. God, oh, how I hate how my heart forgets so easily. I mean, You have been so good to us! You have almost restored me back to life from death!! And here I sit, and I feel unappreciative sometimes, and I forget to ask for help, God! Please help, please don't send more sickness, but maybe that's what we need!

"God, I pray we could be gospel-focused and dependent and never forget about the kindness that You showed us in the hospital. God, please use us to spread Your Word and gospel! I don't know what we are going to do here for the rest of our lives, however long that may be, but please may we not at all be ashamed! But with full courage now as always Christ will be honored in my body, whether by life or by death!"

CHAPTER 17

It's Going to Be So Sweet to See You in Heaven!

April 21, 2017 (*Facebook Update*)

Sometimes, it's hard for me to believe that Matt was lying in a hospital bed, paralyzed and dying just 10 weeks ago. Because today, he walks completely unassisted, talks almost normally, and is much closer to pre-stroke Matt than post-stroke Matt. Today, this post is filled with nothing but good news!

First, the best news. Matt had a PET scan two days ago. It's like a CT scan, but shows the bones as well as the body.

Back in January, the cancer was everywhere. Brain, bones, lungs, abdomen, adrenal glands, etc. Four weeks ago, the cancer had shrunk, but still had remnants everywhere. But as of this scan, there is only one detectable spot in his abdomen with cancer. That's it. No more tumors in his lungs, his bones, or anywhere else in his body.

Oh, there is evidence of the cancer everywhere. Sclerotic lesions of his bones abound where the cancer got in and did damage. But the active cancer has almost completely vanished. The latest data on the drug he's on says that he could continue to respond like this for as long as 29 months. We are hopeful for those numbers and more, but our hope is not in those numbers.

This is not remission really. And it is not a cure. The mutation Matt has is still expected to figure out a way to get around this drug and take control again one day. But it is absolutely a reprieve and a kindness from God that we do not deserve!

Outside of the PET scan and the cancer, Matt's recovery from his stroke is going unbelievably well. This week in physical therapy, he jumped and did a jumping jack. He can put his pants on now one leg at a time, just like everyone else (a real struggle for weeks since standing on one foot requires a lot of balance!). And yesterday for the first time since his stroke, he drove a short distance.

Back on February 18th, when Matt was still in the ICU and had just begun to respond to the drug, I wrote:

"Matt also continues to develop movement in his left hand, another thing for which we are thankful this week. Maybe next week it will be his arm or shoulder or leg, but for today, we are thankful for his hand..."

God has indeed seen fit to restore nearly all that Matt lost. Beyond anything we could have expected or hoped for in this period of time.

Matt is still recovering.

He doesn't have much of an appetite, takes naps most days, and is working hard to regain total control in walking and standing. He trips sometimes. He has ringing in his ears from the radiation almost all the time and sometimes his mind feels cloudy. Things at home are not back to normal the way they were before the stroke. Sometimes, it's tricky because Matt looks so normal that we both expect him to be the same as he was before. He is not yet. He has yet to do the dishes without taking three or more breaks. But the fact he can do them at all (and wants to!) is a gift.

God still has a purpose for us here. It is, I think, so clear that God absolutely wanted Matt to have a stroke and almost die on February 2nd. But I think it is equally clear that He did not want Matt to die that day. Or the following week or the following month. God knows each and every one of Matt's days and he will die exactly when He sees fit, not a day before or after. He knows that day and we do not. So, we will live this uncertain future He has given us the same way we lived through the last couple of months: looking to Him.

God is often glorified in death and suffering, and we may yet glorify Him that way. But today we give Him glory in this reprieve; in this place of joy and hope and healing. He has given us this day with just the same amount of love and power and purpose that He previously

gave us grief and suffering and sorrow. May His goodness be declared in both through two sinners!

Reprieve was the best word for it.

On all fronts, Matt seemed to be doing great.

The PET scan gave us tremendous encouragement! Matt's cancer was about as gone as it could be, with just that one spot in his abdomen remaining.

With these results and Matt's daily improvements, we felt as though we could really try to live again.

Matt could walk, get dressed, and even drive! We were having these sweet dates at outpatient physical therapy and at the gym, drinking coffee together, and talking about what we would do now that God had us in the States instead of Papua New Guinea. We celebrated Easter with our families, shared meals with some of our supporters, and had more family movie nights.

The appetite thing was becoming increasingly a problem, but we were trying to navigate around that. Again, it was difficult to tell if this was a side effect of the Alectinib or something else. Matt was still able to eat; he just didn't feel like it much of the time.

During this time, we began to have conversations about where our kids should go to school now that we would be back in the States and with the potential for me to need to care for Matt, homeschooling seemed less ideal.

Matt, it turned out, felt strongly that they should go to Gilbert Christian, a private school nearby. His life had been so profoundly affected by his time at Northwest Christian School growing up, that if our kids had to go to school, he wanted it to be there.

Now, having been the primary educator of our kids, I also had strong feelings about things like classical education, so I pushed back on more than one occasion. But Matt insisted that what mattered most was not a classical education, but a Christian one.

So, we toured the campus that would eventually become a significant part of our lives.

Matt, his aches and pains becoming more regular and cumbersome and—quite frankly—confusing, still smiled and laughed with the administration and office staff. He readily gave all the glory to the Lord for the joy he had in his present circumstances.

There were no openings at the time because we had four children—nearly all of them had to be wait-listed. But we enrolled them anyway and trusted the Lord.

Enrolling them at that school was the best decision we could have made.

The blessing that Gilbert Christian turned out to be for my kids and myself during the following year is hard to articulate. Suffice it to say, God was already making provision for the kids and for me in what was to come, and this decision was one of the ways He did that.

Had Matt died during his stroke back in February, we never would have had those conversations about schooling and I most likely would not have chosen that school. But he was here, helping me map out a future for our kids.

We did as many family days as we could, although with each passing day Matt seemed to be in a little more pain or discomfort than he was the day before.

Matt wrote:

4/22/2017

"God, it's Saturday, April 22, and we are home. It's a family day. We are hopefully going to go to Fat Cats (a family entertainment center) and then a family movie night tonight. God, please help me with this cancer. Things could take a turn for the worse so easily. Any day could bring bad news.

"But God, I know You are in control of the cancer, and it will not spread past where You want it to. God, please keep me alive, for the sake of my wife and kids, so that I might live to see them graduate high-school, college, get married, have kids, and that we might go on many family trips together.

"But if that was what my life was kept alive for, may it be more than that as well. May I be bold with the gospel and love You and please use me, use us, to make Your Word and gospel known.

"God, please use us. Please give us wisdom about the future and what You want us to do with our lives. God, please give me energy each day to make it through the day and have a happy heart! God, please heal me from the cancer, and please make me a godly man!"

Amidst all the good news, small red flags began to pop up here and there.

For one, Matt's back and stomach pain worsened. It was low-level, but we weren't sure why it was happening at all.

His lack of appetite was also increasingly becoming an issue. This, too, was confusing because his appetite had been normal for the most part in the hospital and throughout rehab. With each day that went by, however, it was becoming more and more scarce.

We knew that cancer can and does suppress the appetite, but having just had the all-clear PET scan, that was the last thing on our minds.

Once again, God knew what we did not.

Although Matt would continue to take it twice a day, the Alectinib had stopped working.

What we had hoped would not happen for another 29 months had already happened: the mutation had figured out a way around the drug, rendering it ineffective.

I didn't know and Matt didn't know.

And so we prayed.

4/25/2017

"God, it's Tuesday and Cameron and I are home reading Your word! God, please help us to have a sweet time reading Your Word now. Please give me grace and strength to wake up earlier and read Your Word! God, please give me energy today for physical therapy as well. I pray that I can work hard, get stronger, and be back to normal someday again! God, please give me my appetite back, please help me to be hungry again, help me to eat enough and eat right—which means giving us wisdom to even know what to eat!

"God, please may the tumors in my brain go away, and please, God, use us while we are here. Please give us wisdom about what to do with the rest of our

lives. Should I get a job, or do GBI (our church's seminary), or pursue something else? God, please provide for us, please make it clear what we should do.

"I do pray, God, that we would continue to be an encouragement to those around us, and that You would continue to use us to make Your gospel known, and that we would be bold with the gospel. Please use us to encourage the saints, our brothers and sisters as well. God, please restore me and help me to be patient—help me to trust You with what You are doing right now. God, please may I be diligent to seek You during this time, and please grow me stronger and stronger in knowledge of You."

Again, undergirding all of his supplications and requests, God was gracious to give Matt a heart that earnestly desired to know Him above all else.

He wanted to grow in the midst of affliction, not shrink. It was God's grace that flowed from Matt's heart to the pages of his journal.

As the cancer continued to grow inside Matt, unbeknownst to us and unchecked without any further resistance from the Alectinib, Matt prayed:

4/27/2017
"God, it's Thursday, and we just heard that Social Security approved me as disabled! God, again, this is a kindness, but I wonder if I should accept it since I actually am less disabled now. But at the same time, maybe this is just your provision for us.

"God, thank You for coffee. Thank You for music. God, thank You for how much You have taken care of us throughout all this. Even when we really haven't been the most faithful, You have just remained faithful and kind to us! Please help us to trust You more, and please bring more things into our life that we can trust You in.

"God, make us godly people in all of this. May we be examples for others and fight hard to know You more and more. God, please provide something for us for the future. Please provide a job of some sort or, God, please provide a direction of some sort. Of course, I'm assuming You are going to keep me alive

many more years. God, so please may You use us here in this place and please heal me from this cancer!

"God, You are a good God, and really none of this is even necessary for us to see Your goodness because You have already demonstrated it for us at the cross!

"Oh, how I look forward to heaven, God. I mean, I want to see my kids grow up and get married, and I want to do more ministry here in this world, but at the same time, it's going to be so sweet to see You in heaven."

It was as though when Matt was handed a terminal diagnosis, the pace at which he was running in life did not slow down but actually sped up.

He still desired to be holy and to know God more and be used for the gospel, even though he had very little appetite, quite a bit of pain, and a body which did not work completely.

Philippians 1:6 says, "And I am sure of this, that he who began a good work in you will bring it to completion at the day of Jesus Christ."

Like a potter glazing, sealing, and sanding his vessel into a finished product, God had begun a good work in Matt Dodd, and He was being faithful to finish it, just as He promised.

MAY-JULY

CHAPTER 18

Make Us Lights in This Dark World!

May 15, 2017 (*Facebook Update*)

This past weekend, I had the privilege of celebrating both Mother's Day and our 12-year anniversary with my husband and kids in California. Both are days I wasn't sure I would get to share with my husband again.

In years past, with both of these celebrations, I would be so self-seeking, so desirous that things go the way I want them to. This year, things went 'wrong' on both those days—Matt was sick on our anniversary and we didn't really do anything on Mother's Day—but I think this year was my very favorite of all anniversaries and Mother's Days because I was just happy to be a part of them, to have Matt a part of them.

I don't deserve to be a mom, to have the sweet kids I have. And I don't deserve to be married to a man who continues to defy all natural expectations and be the same joyful, steadfast Matt Dodd he has always been. A man who, by God's sustaining grace, lifts up his head in the face of obstacles under which one with less of a hope and stronghold would surely collapse. He loves me well and I have had the honor of spending three more months with him than I thought I would have.

I am so thankful that these gifts come from the same good and loving God who both gives them to me and who will one day take them away. He loves my husband and kids more than I ever could and so it is that I can trust Him with them all whole-heartedly. One thing I do know: every day we get together, easy or hard, is a blessing!

In that vein, we are taking a trip.

Lord willing and health permitting, Matt did so great on our trip to California that we have decided to take a cross-country, memory-making, near-coast-to-coast road trip that we are calling "The Dodd-Thankful-We're-Alive Trip!"

Beginning June 5th, we will be traveling through New Mexico, Texas, and Louisiana to spend time with Matt's family and from there, we will continue on to Florida, Georgia, North and South Carolina, Washington DC, and possibly farther up the coast before making our way back to Arizona.

Life is different when you don't know how many summers you have left as a family, and we are so grateful to have this one!! May we be always proclaiming the good things God has done for us whether we are in Arizona or Georgia or Maine (if we make it that far!)!

James 4:13-16 tells us: "Come now, you who say, 'Today or tomorrow we will go into such and such a town and spend a year there and trade and make a profit'—yet you do not know what tomorrow will bring. What is your life? For you are a mist that appears for a little time and then vanishes. Instead, you ought to say, 'If the Lord wills, we will live and do this or that.'"

Similarly, Proverbs 16:9 says, "The heart of a man plans his way, but the Lord establishes his steps."

Matt and I understood these verses.

Especially having gone through the uncertainty that comes with living in Papua New Guinea, we understood that we can make all the plans in the world, but only the Lord's would come to pass.

It was no different when we planned this trip.

The trip to California had been sweet in many ways, mostly just to know that Matt could still take road trips—one of his favorite things! We went to Legoland, the beach, and made family memories.

It was difficult in other ways.

The pain in Matt's stomach and back had been growing steadily and had reached the point where he was uncomfortable sitting down. We chalked the back pain up to still recovering from being bedridden for so long and treated it with various exercises and Tylenol.

The stomach pain we weren't so sure about.

Perhaps it had something to do with a long-term effect of taking the Alectinib?

Matt pushed through the pain to make this the best family trip possible, whether that was making jokes and being silly in the golf cart at Legoland or playing with the kids at the beach.

One of the sweetest moments of those six months happened when Matt called out to me while we were on the beach with our kids.

"Hey, Cameron, watch me!" he yelled.

Off he ran, albeit not very gracefully, on the beach. Not even three months out from a paralyzing stroke and the man was *running* on the beach!

He was thrilled, I was thrilled…it was the answer to the prayer Matt had been praying to be able to run again.

On the night of our twelve-year anniversary, Matt and I ate dinner in a fancy restaurant right on the water in Carlsbad.

The appetizer came out, and Matt ate part of it…and then proceeded to throw it up in the bathroom.

He tried to come back out but was too sick.

I asked for the check and tried very hard to not be anxious.

I was disappointed, of course, in my own hopes for a lovely evening.

But what was steadily creeping into my heart more than disappointment was cold fear.

Matt was a fighter.

If he could have sat through that meal, he would have, which meant that whatever was going on with his body was so bad that he couldn't sit and eat one meal.

I could not fathom that it was the cancer, since it had only been a few weeks since the mostly all-clear PET scan; I simply had no category for cancer returning that fast.

After that dinner, there was a tension in my heart as I watched Matt. I understood that something was wrong with him again, but I did not know what it was.

On the upside, Matt was every day becoming more and more coordinated physically. He was talking and laughing almost the same way as he had before.

This, for us, spoke louder than the low-level pains Matt was having and made us want to take advantage of how well he seemed to be doing while, in our minds, the cancer was under control.

Having gone on one mostly successful family road trip, we began making plans for another.

We mapped out our route and reached out to friends to see where we might be able to stay along the way. I contacted our state Senator to see if we could get a White House tour...we went all out.

Meanwhile, that same prayer Matt had been praying for so many years—that he would not waste his life—he continued to pray.

5/15/2017

"God, it's Monday, and Emily Miles is watching our kids, so Cameron and I can read the Bible. God, please use us during this time to make the gospel known, to make Your Son known. God, please make us bold with Your gospel. God, please heal me from this disease and thank You for this extra time. You could have easily taken me in the hospital, but You had me live longer.

"God, please may I not waste it. Please may I spend every day to its fullest. May I spend and be spent for Your glory. God, I'm sorry about my many past failures and sins. Please, help my back to feel better. Thank You so much God for all that You have brought us through. That I can sit here right now, and type is truly just a miracle in and of itself. God, please use me and if GBI is Your will, I pray that I can excel at it, and learn so much, and be able to minister to many.

"God, please help me to have wisdom about what to do for the future. God, should I become a minister of the gospel? I am a little concerned I won't be able to do it. It's a high calling, and I want to make sure that it's Your will for me, and something that I can accomplish. God, but it would be an honor and a privilege to be able to do that for my life...minister with Your Word. God, please make it clear what we should do. You've provided so much for us...a house to live

in, finances to last a while, a good church, an awesome wife. God, please keep me alive and use me for Your glory."

Matt would, from time to time, take one of our older kids to Starbucks to read their Bibles together and just talk with them about life and the Lord.

One day during this time, he took Benaiah—nine years old at the time—to do just that and prayed while they were there:

5/17/2017

"God, it's Wednesday morning, and I'm sitting in Starbucks with Benaiah. God, please help us to have a good conversation this morning. God, please grow this boy up into a man, and open his eyes that he might know You more and more each day. God, help me to be a good dad to our kids. I feel I'm not quite up to speed after the stroke.

"I don't know how much time I've got; I mean, I could go anytime really. You alone know the answer to this question. You have a plan for us. God, may we just trust You and remain faithful. I do pray that You would keep me alive many more years.

"God, please may I be able to glorify You. I pray for this epic road trip. Please may it all work out, God. Please may we be able to have such a sweet time as a family. God, please may we be faithful and diligent, and serve the body of Christ, even though it's we ourselves who 'need help.'"

     *   *   *   *

Matt's pain levels began to increase at an alarming rate.

And as they did, our conversations about our epic road trip became more and more strained. Our confidence in his ability to sit comfortably for that long—or be comfortable at all—began to waver.

This rapid decline is best illustrated through a snapshot of several entries over the course of the next ten days, as they began to shift more and more in focus from being life-centric to being pain-centric:

5/19/2017

"God, it's Friday morning. Please help my back and body feel better today. God, I pray for this road trip as well, that we would be able to take it and have a good time!

"God, please take care of us, take care of my family. God, please may I love my wife, and care for her. Please help me to be a good husband, and loving father, and good small group participant.

"God, please may we be members of GBC (our church) and encourage others. I get so caught up in my own problems, God, it's like I forget about others. Oh selfish, self-centered man that I am.

God, please use us, please may we be a light for the nations, and for our friends, and family, and please just continue to use us and make us faithful people."

5/20/2017

"God, it's Saturday morning, and I didn't sleep good. My stomach has been hurting for a while, God. I think it's because of the calcium I'm taking, that it's making my stomach hurt. God, please help me to feel better. Really, I haven't felt 100% this whole week.

"God, You are good, please help us to trust You during this time. I pray nothing bad is going on inside, that the pain is not caused by liver failure or something like that, but that it really is just gas, which is what I think it is. Please also can You help my back to not hurt today as well!

"God, I'm sorry that I have not been very faithful these last few weeks. I mean, I haven't been diligent to read Your Word, or pray. Please help me, God; please restore me and make me diligent again! Please help me as I read Your Word now."

5/21/2017

"God, it's Sunday morning, we'll be going to church today. Please help me to not have stomach or back pains.

"God, You are good, and You do good, and this life is so short. I feel like, God, it's harder for me to live life, because I'm either in some low level of pain, or I just have a hard time coordinating everything, or I mentally am not all there.

God, please be gracious today. I don't deserve anything from You, and yet, You have provided so much for us. May we glorify You all along the way. God, please may I be hungry today."

5/23/2017

"God, thank You for another day to be alive. God, my stomach still hurts. God, I don't know why my stomach is hurting. Is it just gas? Or is it something else? You know what's going on. I guess, I'm wondering if I should do something about it? God, please may it stop hurting, please take away the pain, and please may we get to the underlying problem, whatever that may be.

"But God, please help me to not be so self-focused on how I feel, but may I just be able to think about others throughout all this. God, please help me to love others, starting with my wife and kids, and then other people, and not just think, "oh my stomach hurts, blah blah blah". God, please help me. If You could take away the pain, that obviously would make it a little easier, but if not, that's okay; I'll try to learn to deal.

"Thank You, God, that I was able to be hungry yesterday. Thank You that I could eat. God, please help me to be hungry again. God, please help us to love our kids today."

In a matter of days, our conversations about our epic family road trip had gone from being strained to doubtful. Matt's pain and discomfort were not getting better and being in a car for two or three weeks was not going to help it.

By the end of the week, the whole idea was in limbo.

Matt prayed:

5/24/2017

"God, still a strange life we are in. I mean, this morning I woke up and was just in pain and discomfort, and now I'm at Starbucks—feeling good (thankful for Tylenol). God, please give us wisdom on our road trip. I don't know if it would be the best thing if it's going to be so expensive; plus, I'm just not feeling as good as I was. So not sure what we should do. God, I'm sorry I get discouraged.

"Please help me to remember the gospel and remember just truth. I mean, no matter what happens in my day, I'm never getting what I deserve, and I'll never get what I deserve. God, so please be patient with me during this time. Please be patient with me when I forget obvious stuff. God, You have been so good to us. I feel I've just been thinking about myself so much, my pain, and my problems. God, can You please help me to be an example in all of this of a godly man? I'm not sure I've done that since coming home. God, please help me to draw near to You."

With each passing day, Matt's long-held desire to go to seminary to become a pastor became harder for him to visualize.

5/26/2017

"God, it's Friday morning, and my back is hurting again. God, please help me to feel better, please help my back to feel better. Perhaps through stretching, or exercise or something, but please God, take away the pain in my back and stomach.

"God, I don't know what we should do with our lives. God, please continue to use us to reach people. God, please make us lights in this dark world. God, please may I love my wife and love my kids, and care for them well. Please give us wisdom about everything. It's like I want to do GBI, but I honestly don't know if I can do it. I mean, based off of how I feel now, it would be difficult....difficult to get there, and to sit through classes, and to do homework. God, but it would be really awesome to be a minister of the gospel. I don't know if that's what You want for us though. God, please may we be above reproach in everything that we do."

5/29/2017

"God, it's Monday, the 29th of May, and we're thinking of canceling our road trip because of my back and stomach pains. God, I pray that is the best thing to do. God, please give us wisdom about what to do, and how to do it. God, please help my back to stop hurting, and my stomach to stop hurting. God, please may we have a sweet time together as a family. God, please may we be able to draw near to You this summer well."

As Matt's pain began to spike beyond the reach of Tylenol, we took stock of his symptoms.

His back hurt.

His stomach hurt.

He had no appetite and, when he tried to make himself eat, he would gag—unable to get it down. Infrequently but alarmingly, nausea and vomiting had also entered the picture.

Was the appetite suppression caused by the Alectinib?

Was the back pain still lingering side effects of being bedridden?

Was the stomach pain a gastrointestinal problem? An ulcer, maybe?

We weren't sure about anything.

In mid-May, we began troubleshooting the pain with texts to Matt's oncologist and larger doses of Tylenol.

We also scheduled some scans, just to be safe.

Once again, we found ourselves waiting for a scan, trying not to be anxious in the meantime.

5/30/2017

"God, it's Tuesday morning, we are all into a new week, and I'm asking for help. Help with eating, help with not gagging, help with back pain, help with stomach pain, wisdom with travel plans. God, please make the stomach pain stop. Please make the back pain stop.

"God, please help me today to be content and happy even with the pain. God, please help me to read Your Word as well, God, please help me to have a long, encouraging good time in Your Word."

These were troubling times.

There is a passage in the book of John, right before Jesus went to the cross, where he told his disciples:

> *"Let not your hearts be troubled.* Believe in God; believe also in me. In my Father's house are many rooms. If it were not so, would I have told you that I go to prepare a place for you? And if I go and

prepare a place for you, I will come again and will take you to myself, that where I am you may be also."

The disciples' hearts were troubled.

And for good reason! Jesus kept telling them that he was going to leave them, that *he had to go*.

They didn't want Him to go.

Jesus tells them, "Yes, troubling times are at hand. But you don't need to be troubled by them. You can trust that God is still in control and that He is working out a plan of *life* in the midst of the death that is coming".

Jesus had to go.

So that He could secure eternal life. So that He could come back and bring His disciples to Himself. So that where He was, they could be also forever.

In this time of uncertainty, there were whispers of death all around us—in Matt's labs that were beginning to fall again, in his lack of appetite that was slowly turning into vomiting, in his pain that was continuing to escalate.

More and more, it was looking as though Matt was going to *go* when we both wanted him to stay.

Under the Arizona sunshine, the shadow of death stretched its threatening tendrils ever closer to us.

But we knew that the One who had walked through His own shadow of death thousands of years before had done so that our hearts might not be troubled when it was our turn.

We knew that we could trust that He was still in control and still working out a plan of life, even if death were to come. He had promised to bring us to Himself on the other side of this dark valley, that where He was, there we would be also forever!

Matt had prayed this very thing a month before:

"Oh, how I look forward to heaven, God. I mean, I want to see my kids grow up and get married, and I want to do more ministry here in this world, but at the same time, it's going to be so sweet to see You in heaven!"

So, as each step brought us further down into that dark valley, we held these promises in our hands and lifted our heads to the One who had not failed us yet.

And though our hearts were indeed troubled, they also trusted.

That no matter how deep the valley went, that rope of God's faithfulness that had held us through cliff accidents and miscarriages and third-world illnesses would not let us go now. It would keep holding us, just as the Lord had promised, until we made it out on the other side.

CHAPTER 19

Whatever You Do, May We Trust You!

June 3, 2017 (*Facebook Update*)

When we posted a few weeks ago about taking a trip, we used the phrases 'Lord willing' and 'health permitting'.

This is because we know that while we might make our plans, it is ultimately the Lord who knows the future and directs our steps for our good and His glory.

As it has turned out, God knew long before we did that we won't, in fact, be able to take our trip. The good news is that Matt had an MRI last week which came back showing no tumors in his brain. This is incredible, really, since when he was first diagnosed, there were over a dozen. From all that we know, the cancer that once reigned in Matt's body and brain is very much controlled and subdued. Praise God!

But ironically, Matt is actually having more pain now than he has had this entire time. Between back and stomach pains, he has a hard time making it through the day without laying down and being generally uncomfortable. Hence, the cancellation of the road trip. Matt's appetite is also severely oppressed (presumably from the cancer medication) and his ever-present, ultra-sensitive gag reflex that he's had since we've been married makes it difficult for him to make himself eat.

We are troubleshooting what the source of these pains might be and trusting the Lord in the meantime.

As we face these new obstacles, it has been so good to remember what is still true.

Things like we don't deserve to not be in pain. That we will still never suffer as much as Jesus suffered for us. That if God is sovereign over Stage IV lung cancer and complete paralysis on his left side, He is certainly sovereign over stomach pains and back pains and appetite suppression. That the same loving hand that gave us our lives, each other, and our children has now given us cancer, a stroke, and these present difficulties—and still because He loves us!

Philippians 4 says to not be anxious about anything, but that in everything with prayer and supplication and **THANKSGIVING** we are to let our requests be made known to God.

So that is what we're trying to do. Thanking God in the midst of trip cancellations and reduced activity. Praising God in the midst of pain.

Because God is still good and He will never give us more than we can bear.

We did not understand what was going on with Matt's pain.

We were doing our best to control it with maximum doses of Tylenol and Ibuprofen, but each day that went by, they became less effective.

With an all-clear MRI in our hands and an almost-all-clear PET scan only 6 weeks old, we were scrambling for answers.

That Sunday, Matt prayed:

6/4/2017

"God, it's Sunday morning, and I'm sitting on the couch. God, please help me to go to church and just be an encouragement. Please help me to be encouraged in You and encourage my brothers and sisters in Christ. God, please give me the joy of my salvation, the joy of knowing You, which no amount of pain can ever take away!"

We scheduled an ultrasound and CT scan to check for ulcers and the like, and, in the meantime, God was gracious to give Matt some days of lesser pain.

6/6/2017

"God, it's Tuesday morning, and I'm not in that much pain! God, thank You for a morning where I'm not in too much pain. God, please take away all the pain, and please help me to eat. God, I do pray that we would have such a sweet summer together as a family. God, please heal me from this cancer, and make me learn to be content in every circumstance. God, I can do all things through You who gives me strength!"

The day finally arrived for the scans, and we kept pushing forward as we waited for the results.

Matt continued going to the gym because it had seemed to help with his back pain in the past, but this became more challenging as his nausea and gagging increased.

6/7/2017

"God, it's Wednesday, and I didn't pray this morning. God, thank You that we could get everything scanned. Please help me, God, with my pain. I do pray that You would make it so I would have less pain.

"God, You are good, though, and whatever You will for me I will accept. Please give the grace to handle whatever You throw at me though! God, please give the doctors wisdom with everything as they are trying to figure things out. God, please help me to feel better. Please God, sustain my faith and sustain my family during this time, whatever it holds. God, please may we trust in You for everything as well. God, thank You for Cameron and all the work she is doing, thank You for providing such a good helpmate. God, please continue to sustain her through all of this as well. God, please help me to continue to get stronger, head to the gym, and be able to care for my family in whatever little ways that may mean. God, right now as I read Your Word, please convict me of sin, help me to know You more, encourage my heart, and use me during this time to bring praise and glory to Your name, not cursing!"

The not eating began to be more and more of a problem, and I remember being seriously concerned during this time that Matt might starve to death. He wouldn't eat most of the time, and when he would try to eat, he would throw it up.

There are some journal entries that are harder to read than others and the following, for me, is one such entry.

But it is here, in this book, because even in the midst of struggling, Matt still pushed his heart towards thanksgiving and towards praise.

6/9/2017

"God, I haven't eaten much these last 3 days. God, if this is all a result of the stroke, can You please reverse it? God, how different life is now. This makes PNG actually look easier, I think. I would much rather be in PNG with a normal appetite and normal everything preaching the gospel than here, with these issues.

"God, please help me to have a happy heart. Help me to think often of heaven, and often of Your presence. Please help me to eat plenty tonight, please God, may I be able to get a good lunch in. Lord, please give me grace tonight to think that food tastes good again like it used to. God, please may I not get sick. God, please help me to eat and not die. God, please help me to be hungry, please take away the stomach and the back pain.

"God, You are good, and You do good, You have given us so much to be thankful for. I'm thankful for our kids, and for this house we have to live in. God, I'm thankful for our church. God, please may we find a small group to be in. Things I'm thankful for: my wife, oh God, how great a wife do I have? God, I love her so much, and I feel so bad for her having to work so hard during this time, and I feel so worthless just laying on the couch. Thank You, God, though, for such a helper. Thank You for our 4 sweet, beautiful children as well. God, thank You for how You gave them to us, and made them all different. God, please may this medicine take the pain away."

*　　　　*　　　　*　　　　*

June 10, 2017 *(Facebook Update)*

This morning, we received answers about Matt's pain and appetite loss.

And while we are thankful to have answers, it was not good news.

Matt's CT scan yesterday revealed numerous tumors in his liver. The one cancerous lymph node in his last scan had measured one millimeter; it has since grown to nine.

What this means is that, in just over a month, Matt's body stopped responding to the drug he's been taking, and the cancer has quickly taken over. This explains the pain in his stomach and back, as well as his extreme loss of appetite. Due to how aggressive the cancer is and how quickly it's spreading, our best option is to start Matt on chemotherapy on Wednesday.

This is bad news.

Matt and I got to cry with one another one more time this morning as we absorbed information that we were not expecting quite to this degree or quite this quickly. We have always known that chemotherapy was a last-resort option in a terminal illness and moving our feet now in the direction of that path has brought death uncomfortably close.

The road in cancer is like standing on sand, with the ground continuously shifting and sliding out from under you. But the thing about walking the road of cancer for the believer is that underneath all that sand, underneath all that shifting uncertainty, there is a rock that is great and vast and immovable. Should all that sand suddenly fly away, that rock still would not shift, or slide, or move a centimeter.

But more important than its steadfastness for us is that this Rock is good! God gave His own Son for us; how will He not also with Him graciously give us all things? He is a good Father and does not give His children bad gifts, only good ones. These circumstances are no exception.

So we cried this morning—and then we stopped crying.

Because nothing that is truly important has really changed.

God is still on His throne, our sin is still our biggest problem (that has been graciously forgiven in Jesus!), and if there were something better for us than relapse and chemotherapy, He would have given that to us instead. This is the best thing for Matt, the best thing for me, and the best thing for our kids.

Today was a hard day.

The first of many, presumably. Our lives will change a bit. Matt will be sick. He may not be able to be in church every Sunday. Our kids might not be able to play with everyone all the time if sicknesses are around. And our time together as a family might look different. But the fact that we still have time together as a family—even if it's just one day—is a gift that we don't deserve. And for that, we are so very thankful!

Today was a hard day, but it was still a good day. In each of the hardest of external circumstances, there has always been a kernel of joy. So I will close this post with the lyrics to one of my favorite hymns, that Matt and I had our kids read today as we shared the news with them:

"When peace like a river attendeth my way, when sorrows like sea billows roll, whatever my lot, Thou hast taught me to say, It is well, IT IS WELL with my soul."

(Picture below taken today, upon news the cancer had returned.)

It was a Saturday morning when my phone rang.

I had just said goodbye to Matt at the house and was driving somewhere when I picked up.

I knew it wasn't good news because, whatever the results were, his oncologist was calling me with them on a Saturday morning.

With heaviness in his voice, Dr. Polowy told me that the cancer had returned, and that it had done so aggressively.

Multiple new tumors had appeared on the scan, and the one that had been left in his abdomen on the scan in April had grown significantly. The tumors explained the pain Matt was having in his stomach and back. It also shed more light on how aggressive this cancer was, given how much it had spread in just seven weeks.

As he talked, I slowly made a U-turn and began driving back to the house, my heart once again in my throat.

The best numbers at the time for Alectinib gave us hope for twenty-nine months of cancer control.

In God's good plan, Matt got two.

But they were two precious months where he got to recover from his stroke, learn how to walk again, laugh with his family, speak to our church, and then trust God in cancer relapse once again.

We had always known that once the Alectinib stopped working, life expectancy for Matt was not great because the effectiveness of chemo for this type of cancer was not good—if it even worked at all.

I pulled into the garage and turned off the car, thankful that the kids were at homeschool with our friends, and it was just Matt and I at home.

Once again, I would be the one delivering this news to my husband.

Once again, I would look to him for how we would walk through it.

I walked into the house, my heart in my throat, and was greeted with a big smile from Matt sitting on the couch in the living room.

I told him Dr. Polowy had called, and the news was not good.

We sat on that couch, enveloped by sorrow, grappling with the reality that Matt most likely did not have a lot of time left.

We wept together again. Said goodbye again. Reminded each other of what was still true again.

We joked around about it for a moment, and Matt led us once again *towards* God's faithfulness and not away from it. He told me again that he was ready to go, if that was what the Lord wanted.

And somehow, against all human odds, there was still hope in our house that day. There was still peace.

There was still *joy*.

Because we both knew that that One Great Thing had not changed. Matt's life might be lost, but our hope never would.

We scheduled Matt's chemotherapy for the following Tuesday, the first of several, we thought.

In the end, it would only be one.

Matt prayed:

6/11/2017

"God, it's Sunday morning, and I don't feel especially great. God, please help me to fight this, please help me to trust You, because ultimately, there isn't a whole lot I can do to fight this. God, please make the cancer go away, please give me grace to make it through the pain. God, please be gracious to our family.

"God, I pray I could think about the gospel, how I don't deserve anything good. I deserve wrath and punishment from You, and yet, by Your mercy and grace, You saved me and raised me. God, I deserve death, but You have given me life. I deserve Your wrath, but You have given me the riches of Your kindness in Christ Jesus. God, please help me to make it until Wednesday or chemo day with no further complications. Please help me to honor You today at church. May I not be all like, woe is me, but may I just be like, oh, I trust in Him!"

All throughout those months of sickness, I heard Matt say these things.

I heard him declare the Lord's faithfulness, how thankful he was to have this trial and be used in this way.

I saw him being joyful and trusting the Lord. I heard him tell me or the kids that heaven was his home, and he wanted whatever God's will was for his life. And I knew my husband was an honest man.

But there was a part of me that wondered how much of a struggle it was for him internally.

It wasn't until after he died, and I started reading his journals, that I saw just how well God's grace had upheld him. Matt wasn't saying one thing to me or our kids or people who would come and visit, and then, on his own, wrestle with doubts or anger or questions. He kept singing the same song as he had at the beginning, inside and out: God is sovereign, He is good, my hope is in Him alone!

Even in pain, Matt desired to be an encouragement to others and to know God more.

6/14/2017

"God, I don't know how much time I have before the nausea overcomes me, but I don't think I have much in my system. God, please help me to hold it in at least long enough for the pain meds to absorb. God, You are good through all of this, and thank You, thank You for the pain being gone! I mean, life is so different when there is no pain.

"God, please may I trust You in all of this. I pray, God, that we would just be able to encourage others in the midst of this trial. Thank You for the trial, God. Thank You for the opportunity to grow and know You more. Again, strengthen us and sustain us through whatever this may look like. God, please help me today to have a happy heart in You!"

We began chemotherapy in Dr. Polowy's office on a Tuesday, with hopes that it would at least restrain the cancer, in part.

Matt, bless his heart, still didn't like needles, but he always smiled and said thank you.

We tried to keep living life as a family.

We enrolled our kids at Gilbert Christian School, wait-listed and all. Our kids participated in a few summer activities.

All of them did swim lessons. Susanna, our 11-year-old, went to summer camp with our church where the theme was heaven.

She also had a ballet recital she had been working on all year that Matt got to attend—though sitting through it was difficult for him.

Benaiah, our oldest son, gifted in drawing like his daddy, attended an awesome week-long art camp through the school, where he got to express the beauty of God's creation through many different art forms.

Matt would go with me to drop Benaiah off or pick him up, even though he was in so much pain, because Matt, at the end of the day, just loved being with his family.

And he continued to read God's word every day:

6/20/2017
"God, thank You for another day. God, please help me to honor You today. Please help me to grow in knowing You more. God, please take away the anxieties I have right now, including paying for the school year, and just how I'm going to make it out of this chemotherapy without weighing, like, 100 pounds. God, please sustain me, and make me strong, and help me to eat.

"Even now, it's like I'm getting tired, and don't know how long I can read for, but, God, I need Your Word. I mean, it's so, so much easier just to sleep, but then how will my soul be sustained? God, please help us today. Please may Benaiah have a good time at art camp, and please help me to be stronger today, and be able to eat a lot more.

"God, You are good, and ultimately, no matter what happens, God, You are still going to be good. God, thank You that I could keep down some breakfast.

"God, thank You for Moma (Cameron's mom) and the help she has provided us. God, please help us to honor You well in this trial. May the gospel be ever on the tip of our tongue."

Matt's pain levels began to spike again even on the stronger pain meds—not a great sign.

One Saturday, while I took the kids to swim lessons, he prayed about this:

6/24/2017
"God, it's Saturday morning and Cameron is taking the kids to swim lessons. God, please help this pain I have to decrease. I think my biggest concern now is the cancer, and is it wreaking havoc someplace else? I can't see what's going on inside though, and You can, God. God, what's more is You are in control of what's going on inside. God, please help me. Please, God, help me to be healed from this cancer. God, please, for the sake of my family, I pray You would take it all away. God, please help me to love my wife and kids as well.

"God, You are good and the Sovereign God. You created me in my mother's womb. I am wonderfully made. And more though, God, You sent Your Holy

Spirit to remake me. To make me new again. God, please give me a joyful heart in the midst of this, and may we not be afraid of bad news, but may our hearts be firm, trusting in You...why?

"Because, God, we can trust You with our lives and with our cancer. If You want to take me home sooner, then that's the best thing for us. If You wanted to take it all away, You could also. God, please whatever You do, may we trust You."

CHAPTER 20

In Need of Much Grace

June 29th, 2017 (*Facebook Update*)

In many ways, these past few weeks have been as difficult as the first few.

When Matt was in the ICU, it was a volley back and forth between life and death, life and death, until the score settled on life! The trajectory climbed upwards from there so, while still difficult, it was a path filled with things to which we could look forward.

Whereas, since the relapse, it has felt very much like a downward trajectory. Matt's pain continues to increase day by day, despite increased morphine. His fatigue also persists, as does his appetite suppression. Matt's oncologist is not concerned so much with the elevated pain as he is with what it indicates about the cancer activity within his body.

Where all of this leaves us is hoping in the Lord.

In the midst of these circumstances, it is as though the promises of God—and Jesus Himself!—is this Rock to which I am tethered, surrounded on all sides by the waves of our circumstances. Sometimes they are only ripples, sometimes they are daunting swells.

There are days when I believe things so strongly that it's like I am standing on this Rock, barely touched by the water's spray. There are other days when all I can manage is to do is cling with my fingertips to this Rock that will not let me go. And there are still other days when my sorrow and anxieties have me jumping off the Rock and flailing about in the waves. But even then, the Rock is still tethered to me.

Ultimately, the practical realities of this disease are ugly and difficult--watching Matt lose weight, watching him be sick for so long, watching sleep absorb more hours of his day than being awake. But the eternal realities of our circumstances have not changed. And they are all good news!

Susanna, our oldest, called me in last night to talk about Matt. Our conversation went like this:

"Mom, Dad doesn't play with us anymore."
Me (wincing because of how marked by playing with his kids Matt was prior to the stroke): "I know. I'm so sorry, Susanna. That's the cancer."
Susanna (crying): "I don't want him to die."
Me (climbing into her bunk bed with her and crying myself): "I know. I don't want him to die either."
Susanna: "What about Mary? She won't remember him."
Me: "She might forget some things about him, but she'll remember others. We might forget some things about him, too, but we will remember lots of things. But Susanna, (straightening and drying my tears) let's put our eyes where they need to be in this. Where do they need to be?"
Susanna: "On heaven?"
Me: "Yes! If Dad dies, the Bible tells us that that is only gain for him. He will gain everything and lose nothing! We might lose something for a little while, but for him it is only gain."

And my sweet, little eleven-year-old nodded, dried her tears, and was by God's grace able to go to sleep with a smile on her face.

Matt—mercifully forgiven and unequivocally loved by His Creator, Sustainer, and Friend—will gain heaven one day. And on that day—be it tomorrow or 50 years from now—he will have not lost a thing. To be in the presence of Jesus is worship, rest, pleasure, and joy.

So we continue to fight as hard as we can for him to live as long as God might want him to live, but also prepare our hearts if the time for him to go comes sooner rather than later. And in that fight, that has grown harder in recent days, we fix our eyes where they need to be and

where our hope is: Jesus, who suffered to purchase our forgiveness; who lost for a time that we might gain for eternity.

The chemo wasn't working.

Even with the stronger pain medication Matt had been prescribed, the pain was still breaking through—an indication that the cancer was likely spreading unrestrained.

During this time, Matt began sleeping more and looking less healthy. He interacted with the kids less and less and seemed in some ways to be physically shutting down.

We were hopeful, of course, that the chemo might have a delayed effect in pushing back the cancer, and so we waited to see.

Matt's habit since the day I met him was to wake up and read the Bible first thing in the morning.

He would grab his computer, open Logos (the Bible application on his computer), type a prayer to help focus his heart, and then spend time reading and studying God's word. That is where much of this book has come from: those years of faithfully writing down or typing up his prayers each morning.

On June 29th, 2017, he did this for the last time.

In his weakness, he faithfully opened his computer, went to Logos, and this is what he wrote:

6/29/2017

"God, it's Thursday morning and I'm feeling nauseous. I'm not sure why. God, I do pray that this chemo works—that You would save me from this cancer. God, please be gracious to me and heal me, and please if not, please take care of my family while I am gone! God, please give me the strength now to not throw up and to not think about my pain. God, You have been so good to us already, we don't need any more grace from You, but at the same time God, we do need much grace from You!"

This was not Matt's last prayer, of course.

Nor was it his last conversation or his last smile or his last hug.

But looking at these words on his computer screen…and seeing no more after them meant the end of something on this earth for him.

Over the next few days, Matt's pain would sharply increase, collapse in all around him, and cause him to be hospitalized.

As aggressive as we thought his cancer was, it was more so.

Matt's race on this earth was coming to an end, and he desperately needed grace to finish.

In Exodus 2, when Israel is groaning because of their slavery under Egypt, they cry out for help. Verse 24 and 25 says, "And God heard their groaning, and God remembered his covenant with Abraham, Isaac, and with Jacob. God saw the people of Israel—and God knew."

God hears the cries of His people.

And because He is faithful, He remembers His promises to them, and He *acts*. Sometimes, He delivers them from the trial; sometimes, he strengthens them in it. Very soon, Matt would walk through the shadow of death, but he would not be alone.

On this terrible day of pain, God saw Matt—and He knew.

CHAPTER 21

See You in Heaven!

July 5, 2017 (*Facebook Update*)

Two days ago, Matt was admitted to the hospital due to his increased pain, nausea, and fatigue. After a CT scan of his chest and abdomen, we found that the cancer has spread significantly since the scan that was taken just three weeks ago.

When Matt's sweet and wonderful oncologist sat down with us with the results from the CT, he said that Matt likely has four weeks left to live.

So.

In light of this soul-aching news of the Lord taking Matt soon, I'd like to tell you about all the things He has given us.

Matt should have died on a remote mountaintop in Papua New Guinea when he had his stroke back in February. We should have been alone, in a village, completely at a loss for what happened or why. But instead, God had Susanna get sick with tonsillitis, over and over again, so that we would come home--so that we knew about the cancer, so that doctors would save his life in February, so that we would have the last six months together as a family.

In those six months, God has given us a house to live in, furniture to sleep on, and insurance to pay our staggering medical bills. We've gotten to run on the beach, celebrate another anniversary, and watch our daughter turn eleven together.

But we look back further than that.

We can look back to when I fell off a cliff in 2005 and God spared my life.

We can look back to the last 13 years together (really our whole lives!), where God has never once failed to provide food for us to eat, clothes for us to wear, or a roof over our heads—even if it was just a hut when Matt was hiking all over the non-sanitized mountains of the equatorial jungle.

We can look at our four really stupendous kids and the time He has given us to watch them grow up until this point. As a result, they all have a bit of Matt in them and that is something precious God didn't have to give us.

And we can look back further than that—to a day where Roman soldiers put a convicted man on a cross who would not and could not stay dead. Where Jesus bore the sins of everyone who would look to Him to be saved, and then rise from the dead as a promise and a hope. That if He be raised, so shall we—not just to streets made of gold or gates made of pearls, but to the One who made us, gave His Son to redeem us, and sustains us until the day He appoints for us to be with Him.

God has given us salvation and eternal life through Jesus Christ! For us to begrudge or bemoan this news is just silly. Sad, yes. Sorrowful and difficult and filled with grief. But not wrong, not unjust, not unkind, not unloving. If anything, we have seen the opposite of that.

It has been the heaviest of days.

I have had to tell those four sweet children that they will need to say goodbye to their daddy. And I have had to process the fact that one day soon, the goodbye Matt and I say to each other will really be our last.

It has been hard not to dwell on the fact that more than losing anything else Matt has been to me over the last 13 years, I will lose my best friend.

These things are true and real and unspeakably hard to wade through.

And yet.

There is an 'and yet'.

And yet, I will see Matt again. And yet, the things that were true last week are still true. God is still good and faithful and worthy to be praised! Our sin is still forgiven! He has done us no wrong in bringing

Matt to death the same way He brought him to life. And the fact that there is an eternity of joy with Jesus waiting for him in a matter of weeks is just mercy and grace we have never and could never deserve.

So we are weeping. And grieving. And talking about hospice and miracles and end of life preferences. But then we lift up our heads.

Because all is not lost.

My treasure and my kids' treasure is ultimately not found in Matt. We have it yet. And that Treasure will hold us and sustain us now the same way He has every day up until this point. Perhaps more so now. Because He knows what it is to be a father and a husband. He is the father to the fatherless and the defender of widows and it is His joy that is now our strength.

God may yet want Matt alive for another 50 years, but medically speaking, we are preparing for much sooner than that. So with Job we say, "Naked we came from our mothers' womb and naked shall we return. The Lord gave, and the Lord has taken away; blessed be the name of the Lord."

There have been a handful of surreal moments in my life.

Moments where I felt as though I was wading through time, disbelieving it was actually happening.

That night in the hospital, when Dr. Polowy sat across from me with a sedated and unconscious Matt in between us, and said the words, "four weeks to live" was another.

Two days before the hospital, Matt's pain levels intensified.

It got to the point where Dr. Polowy told us to take him to the emergency room. Matt was having a really hard time on the way there and, by the time we pulled up to the doors, was in a full-on pain crisis. He began vomiting, unable to get out of the car because he was so sick.

Dr. Polowy rushed to our aid behind the scenes, completing all the check-in work for us so that as soon as we got him out of the car, the nurses were able to take him straight back without us having to wait.

It took hours to get the pain under control, which, in the end, was only achieved by sedating him.

I had on some level expected this news since that first MRI scan back in January.

I knew it was a terminal illness; I knew those words would have to come one day.

But knowing they will come and actually hearing them are two different things. I tried to think of what questions I was supposed to ask or what the right words to say were to a pronouncement like that.

But in the end, I had none.

Throughout Matt's illness, I had to tell him he was dying on three separate occasions. The news always came to me first.

First, after the results of his biopsy.

Second, after Dr. Polowy told me the cancer had come back.

And now, looking at Matt laying in that hospital bed, I knew I would have to tell him for a third and final time.

I couldn't tell Matt at the moment because he was unconscious.

I could, however, tell others that needed to know.

His mom, his sister, my family, our co-workers in Papua New Guinea.

There is something terrible and real when you tell other people news like this, but it has to be done.

Meanwhile, I was desperately trying to understand what the word 'hospice' meant.

The part of me that wanted to keep fighting for Matt asked for a hospice provider that would allow Matt one more blood transfusion at home for his dropping platelets. This allowance was never used, however, as it would have just prolonged the physical suffering Matt was enduring. But they sent him home with a PICC line (a tube running from a vein in his arm all the way to his heart), just in case.

Eventually, after a full two days, Matt was cognizant enough for me to tell him that Dr. Polowy had given him four weeks to live.

Matt's response while still heavily medicated was, "That's not a lot of time."

Of course, God knew that the timeline Dr. Polowy had given us was incorrect.

Matt did not have four weeks left to live.

He had two.

We spent five days in the hospital as the doctors worked hard to get Matt's labs stable enough for him to be discharged while I worked things out with hospice.

Friends and family kept us company.

People began to come by the hospital to say their goodbyes to Matt. My mother was my near-constant companion; an always-reliable source of friendship, love, and support.

Matt was discharged and made it home with a strong enough dose of morphine to manage the pain while still allowing him to be lucid.

Even with the morphine and the pain, Matt was still himself.

Still made jokes.

Still talked about the Lord.

Still had joy.

It was a remarkable thing to see such steadfastness of spirit despite every physical resource he had shutting down.

From the day he was discharged, Matt would have only nine conscious days left on this earth.

But he still would not waste them.

July 12, 2017 *(Facebook Update)*

I walked cemeteries yesterday to find a place to bury my husband.

I didn't walk alone and there was kindness along the way, but there are some walks that cannot be made easier no matter how pleasant the breeze.

Matt was discharged home from the hospital last Friday, July 7th, in the care of hospice. Our goals have changed drastically from what they once were: from aggressive treatment and fighting to prolong Matt's life to acknowledging the overtaken-by-cancer state God has ordained for Matt's body and doing everything we can to make him comfortable.

The rapid decline we've seen just from last Friday has been difficult to watch. Matt has returned to the wheelchair he fought so hard to get out of; he doesn't really eat anymore; swallowing water has again become a daunting task.

But would you believe it if I told you he still has joy?

It has become more and more apparent that the joy that Matt has is totally untethered to anything on this earth—not to his physical body, not to his earthly aspirations, not even to his family.

The joy that Matt possesses comes solely from the Lord and persists even as all else is giving way. It is joy that is founded and grounded in knowing that—come what may—his sin is still forgiven and the Good Shepherd that laid down His life for him will not lose a single one of His sheep.

As believers, we tell each other that this world is not our home; that we are pilgrims and sojourners here, watching and waiting for a better country. After a life spent watching and waiting for that country and its King, in whom is all our hope and joy, Matt is now just steps away from it.

There is grief in this place.

And so much sorrow that it hurts physically when I look right at it.

I sat across from a kind gentleman today and listened as he described how the funeral home would come to pick up Matt's body when the time came. I listened and finished making arrangements because, as emotionally compromised as I might be now, I will be more so soon and want to be as clear-headed as possible to make such permanent (and expensive!) decisions.

The weight and burden of what is and what is coming is heavier in some moments more than others.

I sent the kids in one-by-one to say goodbye to their dad the other day and heard him exhort each one to seek the Lord and for the older ones not to worry about me because the Lord will take care of me.

There are hours that feel like days where I get brief-but-wonderful interactions with Matt followed by long periods of sleeping. I have wept intermittently as dear friend after dear friend has said their goodbyes to this remarkable man.

I have done impossible things these past few days.

But I would be remiss to leave it there.

Because even as I write and weep in recounting these things, my heart is pulled back and settled in quite a wonderful place of peace.

When we got saved, did we not give our lives to the Lord? Did we not say, "Our God is in the heavens; He does all that He pleases" and rejoice that that is, in fact, true?

Because we believe and trust that God knows better than we do, that He is infinitely more merciful, gracious, and good, and therefore we WANT Him to do what pleases Him. Though it come at great cost to us, we would gladly have His will done in our lives.

And that confidence—that these things are, in fact, good; that the character and promises of God are so unalterable and infallible that we can rest in His unfailing love on our weariest days of dealing with cancer—that, I suppose, is what faith is. How precious is the One who gives such faith as to sustain a dying man and his grieving wife!

When I asked Matt earlier today in a brief moment of awareness what he would have me write from him on Facebook, he said with his eyes closed, "Tell them that I'm still strong in some ways though my body is getting weaker."

I would say the same thing. We are still strong, though weak in so many ways, because the strength is not ours. It comes from the One whose strength is made perfect in our weakness.

(Picture taken yesterday with Matt's friend Jacob Hantla, after which he said, "See you in heaven, Jake!")

What I remember from these days is a flurry of busyness, sorrow, and joy.

The busyness came from friends and family who came to say goodbye. Matt's family and others, each interaction more difficult to watch than the last.

Matt's longtime friend, Jake, flew in for a night from California where his own son was undergoing treatment for leukemia.

He said goodbye to Matt and then took a selfie with both of them smiling, after which Matt smiled and said, "See you in heaven, Jake!"

Another highlight from this week was having some very dear friends of ours from Countryside Bible Church in Dallas fly in to say goodbye. Matt, in his reduced state, was so encouraged by their visit. We got to pray together and praise God together.

Matt's joy, despite everything, did not waver.

There were still challenging moments. It became harder and harder for Matt to walk with balance. It became harder and harder for him to drink water without choking on it. The wheelchair returned, and Matt stopped eating entirely right around the time he came home from the hospital.

Those obstacles we had worked so hard to overcome after the stroke were now insurmountable.

One morning, as I was helping him to the bathroom and back, he told me that sometimes, when the pain was excruciating, he would pray that God would let him die.

"Do you think that's wrong?" he asked.

I told him there was a reason we had a 'Do not resuscitate' sign on our fridge; why we weren't giving him another blood transfusion. Through tears, I told him that he could go; that I didn't need him to stay anymore. I told him how much I loved him, but that the kids and I would be fine—he could go, if that's what God wanted.

We had been so blessed to be able to say goodbye to each other throughout the last six months. That was the last time we got to do it.

God knew how hard that conversation was for me.

The last six months had been a fierce battle in my heart between loving Matt so much that I would fight any insurance, any bureaucracy, any red tape to preserve his life; I would learn how to be an ICU nurse, a lawyer, or a pharmaceutical rep to get Matt the care he needed so he could stay here with us a little longer.

And yet—as I was doing all those things with all my might, I was still trying to hold him as loosely as I could, knowing that it might very well be God's will for him to die.

For me, telling Matt it was okay to die that day was one of the hardest things I have had to say as a wife because there was such a big part of my heart that wanted him to stay.

But I didn't want him to be in pain anymore, and I did want the Lord's will to be done more than mine—and it was looking more and more like that was for Matt to die.

We were walking two different roads, Matt and I.

But we clung to the same rope, and it continued to hold us fast.

CHAPTER 22

We Can Still Rejoice!

July 18, 2017 (*Facebook Update*)

At noon today, Matt breathed his last in this world and woke up in the next.

The moment came after four days in a near-comatose state, about four days longer than what hospice predicted. We spent our time since Saturday watching and waiting with Matt for the time God had appointed before he was born to be with Him in heaven until, at last, it arrived.

There was nothing pleasant about watching him die, except for the sweet fact that I was able to be with him. In fact, in God's providence, despite being literally surrounded by friends and family nonstop for the last few days, I was alone with a stranger from hospice when the time came.

There were a few terrible, fearful moments right afterwards as I was alone with his body where I wondered if I would be able to live my life in the Lord without Matt just as strongly as God had enabled me to with him. It felt---for a brief and terrible moment—like I had lost everything.

So I picked up my Bible and, alone in my room, read passages that just hours before I had read to Matt to encourage him. I realized that these verses I could now read just to my own soul—verses like, "God is our refuge and strength"!

I thought about how the things that I so dearly loved about Matt were really only tangible reflections of who God is—His love and joy and humility and kindness—and that, lo and behold, I still have Him! And therefore, I still have everything.

Matt's joy today is unmixed. He is where he has longed to be since he became a Christian back in junior high. He is with the Source of his love and joy and hope and thusly, we weep not for where he is now.

We weep rather for where we are still—here in this broken world without his reflection of God's joy and love and hope. There is a place in my heart reserved for Matt that now feels vacant and I feel that space more deeply than I can quite put into words.

But the thing is, there is still joy and love and hope even in this broken world because Matt was not the source of it—God is. And that life and light he so exuberantly radiated were never rooted in him, but in Christ! And the God of Matt Dodd is still my God; the Savior and Sustainer of my husband's heart is the same Savior and Sustainer of my own heart.

So the sorrow in this house is palpable and the abrupt change in our family seems unbelievable at times in its scope. But there is still quiet joy and hope undergirding the entire structure of our family—my kids' prayers today reflected that.

We will sing and laugh and dance in this house again.

Maybe not today.

Maybe not for a little while. But one day.

Because all is not lost. Matt is already saying 'light and momentary'. He is already declaring death gain and absence from the body presence with the Lord. And we rejoice for him and with him.

And we also weep. And hold each other's hands as we look to a tomorrow that will be very unlike today. But mostly, we look to the Lord and His good and infallible purposes and say with George Mueller, "The Lord was good and did good in giving Matt to us; the Lord was good and did good in leaving him with us for so long; and the Lord was good and did good in taking him from us".

We did not know when it would happen.

Hospice had told us on Friday night that Matt could die anytime—possibly even that night. He slept more and more and no longer came out of his room to sit in the recliner in the living room.

But Matt was an otherwise healthy, 36-year-old male, and his heart was strong. Strong enough to keep him alive for four more days.

It was a difficult last few days.

As the hours wound down, Matt's pain seemed to increase.

Even on an unlimited supply of morphine, he would still groan and cough that awful wet cough, each one sounding as though it might be his last.

One night, he began coughing like that, and I just put my hand on his face and said, "You're doing such a good job. I'm so sorry."

Without opening his eyes, Matt, perhaps more from habit and a sweet disposition than actual consciousness, said, "It's not your fault."

There were difficult moments.

But oh!

Can I tell you some wonderful ones?

The first came in the form of a phone call from the vice-principal—now my dear friend—of the Gilbert Christian Schools campus where our kids were enrolled, but waitlisted. She said that the entire office staff was so impacted by Matt and his joy the day we toured the campus that they had been praying for four spots to open up...and they had.

It was such good news! And the first person I wanted to share it with, of course, was Matt. I tried to tell him, but he wasn't really responsive in that moment. So instead, I just rejoiced inside and praised the God who does not give us more than we can bear with His strength.

Another wonderful thing God provided during these days was two very sweet, very special friends.

Keeping vigil and watching for someone to die is not a pleasant task.

Matt would sometimes wake up vomiting or, towards his last days as he slept more, cough this terrible cough as his lungs began to fill with fluid. God provided two dear men, friends of mine and Matt's, to come over at night and stay up through the night with him, while my mom and I slept in the living room.

They would read Scripture to an unconscious Matt, pray with him, and watch with him for the time God had for him to go home. These men were such gifts to me because they spared me many moments of watching Matt suffer, and they allowed me to rest during a time where very little of it was to be found, day or night.

But the best gift that God gave me in the days leading up to Matt's death was his last conversation.

One of those sweet two men, our friend, Kyle Frazey—whose family had opened their home for us to live with them both before we went to Papua New Guinea and when we had come back— was on vacation in Hawaii with his family when he called to check in on Matt. I told him that I didn't think Matt would still be alive when he got back.

So Kyle caught a red-eye flight back home to say goodbye.

He came to our house on Saturday, and it was with this dear friend that Matt would have his last conversation.

It was hard to know at this time how Matt was doing.

He slept so much of the time and was in pain the rest. He wasn't talking as much; he could no longer read the Bible.

Was he okay?

Was he scared?

Angry? Worried? Sad?

"Matt," I gently shook my husband's shoulder to wake him on Saturday morning. "Kyle is here. He flew back from Hawaii to say goodbye."

I wasn't sure if he would wake up.

And even if he did, I wasn't sure he would have any energy to have a conversation.

So I shook him, not knowing what the result would be.

Matt opened his eyes, rolled over to face Kyle, and greeted him with more energy than I had seen him have in days.

As I left the room to give them a moment, I heard Matt say with enthusiasm these eternally glorious, truth-filled, soul-sustaining words:

"But Kyle, we can still rejoice! We have an inheritance that is imperishable, undefiled, and unfading, kept in heaven for us!"

In the throes of death, Matt's thoughts were filled with life.

1 Peter 1:3-8 says,

"Blessed be the God and Father of our Lord Jesus Christ! According to his great mercy, he has caused us to be born

243

again to a living hope through the resurrection of Jesus Christ from the dead, **to an inheritance that is imperishable, undefiled, and unfading,** kept in heaven for you, who by God's power are being guarded through faith for a salvation ready to be revealed in the last time.

"In this **you rejoice**, though now for a little while, if necessary, you have been grieved by various trials, so that the tested genuineness of your faith—more precious than gold that perishes though it is tested by fire—may be found to result in praise and glory and honor at the revelation of Jesus Christ.

"Though you have not seen him, you love him. Though you do not now see him, **you believe in him and rejoice with joy that is inexpressible** and filled with glory, obtaining the outcome of your faith, the salvation of your souls."

It was as if, for just a moment, Matt Dodd became the living embodiment of these words.

Matt's hope still lived, though he was about to die.

Death was coming, but so was his inheritance in Christ!

Just like that passage in James 1, Matt had been counting this trial joy because of what he *knew* was true: that the testing of his faith was actually making it more steadfast.

And here, at the end, he did the same thing: counting his circumstances joy—not because of what he felt, but because of what he *knew.*

Though he was grieved at leaving his family, being in physical pain, and facing death, Matt knew that what was coming was far better than what he was leaving.

That this "light and momentary affliction" was preparing for him "an eternal weight of glory beyond all comparison" (2 Corinthians 4:17).

That one day very soon his lowly body would be transformed to be like Jesus' glorious one (Philippians 3:21).

But most of all, Matt knew that one day very soon he would see his Savior.

He had not seen Jesus, but he had loved Him since he was 13 years old.

Though he couldn't see Him now, Matt believed in Him and rejoiced with joy that was inexpressible and filled with glory, that he was about to obtain the outcome of his faith—the salvation of his soul!

Matt's hope was never staked on doctors or statistics or the efforts of his wife.

His whole hope was in the Person and work of Jesus Christ…and He was about to see Him!

His hope, his joy, could not be shaken because Jesus was the source of it, and He never is.

Matt reminded Kyle of the reason why they could still rejoice, and then he charged Kyle to preach the gospel, since he would no longer be here to do it.

That is what Matt Dodd was thinking about in the last hours of his life.

His hope in heaven.

Preaching the gospel.

And there was still *joy*.

When I had read that woman's article so many years ago, I was sure that the gospel should be enough to handle any tragedy.

And here I was, seeing Matt prove that to be true.

Rather than look to that woman's response difficulty, I looked to George Mueller's.

George Mueller served as a faithful pastor and evangelist in Bristol, England, for sixty-six years, founding five much-needed orphan houses. He had been married to his beloved wife, Mary, for 39 years when she passed away, and it was he who preached her funeral sermon a few days later.

His text was Psalm 119:68: "You are good, and you do good," and this was his outline:

1. The Lord was good, and did good, in giving her to me.
2. The Lord was good, and did good, in so long leaving her to me.
3. The Lord was good, and did good, in taking her from me.

This is what I prayed my heart would be when the time came for Matt to be with the Lord.

And in God's timing, that day was fast approaching.

*　　　　*　　　　*　　　　*

No amount of theology makes death less painful or more endurable.

As those tendrils of death stretched ever nearer, Matt's body showed new evidence of it every day.

His belly that had not had any food in many days began to swell larger and larger, before settling back down. His skin began to change colors. His face grew very pale.

Death is not pretty.

And waiting for it to arrive is not easy.

But one day, arrive it did.

It was Tuesday, July 18th, 2017.

Having had so many hours pass by with no change, I wasn't sure how much longer it would be. Hospice had been sending someone over periodically to help me wash Matt and change him.

That morning was one of those times.

People had been coming and going almost nonstop for days, and there was always someone around to help wash my dishes or do my laundry or play with my kids. It was such a sweet expression of the body of Christ.

My mom, my near-constant companion, was all but glued to my side in those days. She would eat with me, sleep with me, cry with me, rejoice with me. She was my buddy.

So it was that she was with me and this gentleman from hospice as we began to bathe Matt.

As we did, the gentleman from hospice began talking about how much he didn't understand Christians. He didn't know, I don't think, that I was a Christian.

He told me story after story of how in his line of work, he had often seen Christians die and watched how their family members had occasionally rejoiced in that moment.

This gentleman looked me in the eye and said, "That's when I realized that they had lost their humanity."

He then continued with the task at hand.

All the while that this guy is talking, my husband is undressed, without much physical dignity, and I'm just thinking, "Man, I should share the gospel with this guy, but maybe not right now. Maybe after Matt's dressed or something."

And then the doorbell rang.

My mom stepped out to get it.

The hospice worker and I rolled Matt onto his side as we continued to bathe him…

…and Matt exhaled.

I froze because the sound was unlike anything I had ever heard.

The hospice worker across from me went still.

And I knew.

Matt had just taken his last breath.

I was confused for a moment, because afterward there was a tiny inhale, but one glance at the hospice worker told me what I needed to know.

Matt was about as disgraced physically as one could be, and that was the moment he was gone.

Of all the times I would have chosen not to be alone—of all the times I would have chosen to have someone with me, reminding me of truth, and holding me up—here I was, alone with this hospice worker.

A man who not only seemed to really not like Christians, but who had just finished talking about how inhumanely Christians responded to their loved ones dying.

I was suddenly very self-conscious of how to respond.

Not that I knew how to respond; I didn't.

Matt was gone.

It was so obvious from his face, his body. In an instant, everything that made Matt *Matt* had vanished.

My husband was not here anymore.

"What do I—" I began.

"No, no—you just stay by him," he said, gesturing to Matt's face, working quickly and now silently to finish his job.

Stay by him? I thought. *But he isn't here anymore. I can't wake him, can't talk to him anymore, can't comfort him.*

Inevitably, the man needed my help to get Matt clean and dressed. We worked quickly, and then folded his hands and closed his eyes.

Then the hospice worker gathered the trash and left, closing the door behind him. I sat alone, next to Matt's body, reeling in disbelief.

Suddenly, I was terrified.

Like a bottomless abyss, fear and terror opened in blackness before me. I felt as though I was dangling above this abyss, trying with all my might to hold onto that same rope I always had to keep from falling in.

I was uncertain about everything.

I had never been a Christian without Matt.

I got saved after I met him and had always had him to lead me, teach me, pull me back when I wandered too far.

Could I do this without him?

Would I lose my faith?

Was any of it real for me without him?

Would I, right here in this moment, lose everything?

Fear filled every nook and cranny in my heart, and my grip on that rope began to give way.

I didn't have Matt there anymore to hold onto me.

One of my fingers peeled off.

Maybe it was only his strength that had kept me holding on for all these years.

The rest began to slip.

I was vulnerable; I was alone.

I let go.

At a loss to do anything else, I reached for my Bible.

Without feeling anything, I flipped to the passage I had just been reading to Matt hours before.

When he was still alive.

I read Psalm 46:1-2: "God is our refuge and our strength, a very present help in trouble. Therefore we will not fear though the earth gives way, though the mountains be moved into the heart of the sea."

There was nothing mystical about this passage. No miraculous voice from heaven or illuminated words on a page.

It was just truth.

And as I read, there came in this quiet assurance that these things were still true. That my faith had never been tethered to Matt, but to this. And that though I had lost Matt, I had not lost this.

I realized in that moment that though I wasn't holding onto the rope anymore, it was still holding on to me.

It had not let me go.

Slowly, it was as if the Lord just reached down and quietly closed that abyss of fear and terror.

I was alone in a room with my husband's body…and the Lord met me there.

He saw me. Like the Israelites in Egypt. Like Hagar in the desert. Like the widow of Nain. God saw me; He knew.

I realized that Matt didn't need to hear this verse anymore, I did, and it was still true for me!

God was *my* refuge and my strength.

Of all the ways I might have imagined the moment of Matt's death, the way it actually happened was much harder.

But God's purpose never errs.

Had I not been so alone and so disturbed, had I had my mom by my side like always, I would have run to her for help.

But I was alone, and all I had in that moment was my Savior.

And He did not let me go.

Isn't that wonderful?

Eventually, I had to leave the room. Someone had to tell my kids that their daddy had died, and it was going to be me.

I took a deep breath, asked God for mercy and grace one more time, and I left the room. I avoided the eyes of all in the house, went straight to the kids' room where they were playing Legos, and told them that Daddy had died.

They all froze and looked at me.

"Can we see him?" Susanna asked.

"You want to see him?" I said, confused and slightly horrified. "I don't think you want to. He doesn't look the same. He looks different."

"We want to see him," they all insisted.

And so we went, walking past the people in my house and into my bedroom.

We entered the room, and there was Matt's body, already looking stiffer and less natural than even a few minutes before. I let them look at him for a moment before I herded them onward like sweet, little ducklings past the bed and into my walk-in closet, closing the door behind us.

I sat us down in a circle on the floor and talked to them about what was still true.

"Where is Daddy right now?" I asked, tears rolling down my cheeks.

"Heaven," they replied.

"That's right," I agreed. "He's with Jesus right now, rejoicing in His presence. He's not in pain anymore. We are still here, but, you guys, is God still good? Can we still trust Him?"

They nodded, tears now filling their eyes.

"Listen," I said, my voice breaking as I looked at my children, more aware of what they had lost than they were, "we don't have Daddy anymore. But we still have Jesus! And if your Daddy was here, he would be telling us that that is far better. If God thought it was better for him to still be here, then he would be. This is the Lord's will; it is the best thing for Daddy and the best thing for us."

Somewhere inside I knew that the baton for leading this family had just been passed to me.

That it was now me these little ones would look to for the response to bad news that would determine how we walked through it. I didn't have the strength to carry the weight of that baton on this day, but I knew that my God would lend me His. And He did.

I took a deep breath, still crying, but voice steady now.

"Daddy is gone, but we are still here. God still has a purpose for us *here*. So, we are going to cry because we miss him, and then we are going to lift our heads and keep walking because God is in control of this, He is good, and we can trust Him, okay?"

Four small heads nodded.

We went around the circle and took turns praying. They prayed such sweet, thankful prayers, even four-year-old Mary.

Susanna prayed, "Lord, thank you that Dad is now in heaven with Noah (our miscarried baby) and the other Noah (from the ark). And Lord, please also be with the Caruso family at church whose mom is also sick with cancer. Make her better, Lord, if it's your will, and give them strength to go through what they're going through like You've given us strength."

We sat on that closet floor, crying and praying together for a few more minutes. Then we dried our tears, stood up, and left the room together.

The worst of the moment had passed.

That day, a line was drawn in the sand. Moving forward, my life would forever be divided into two halves: that with Matt in it and that without; people who knew him and people who didn't.

Now came the beginning of everything else.

I told my mom and everyone else that Matt was gone, and the machine that is hospice protocol began.

Kind friends kept my children company as I made necessary phone calls and waited for the funeral home people to arrive with the hearse.

I watched, unnerved, as hospice workers quickly, and without my permission, poured all Matt's morphine down my kitchen sink, until I realized that that was probably a wise preventative measure in a lot of households.

As I waited, my pastors began to arrive.

I had asked in the days leading up to Matt's death if any of my pastors might be available to come and pray with me when the moment came.

I didn't know what it would be like when he died, but I knew that when it did, I wanted to be like Job on the day he lost everything. And like David when his child died.

I knew I wanted to worship.

When Job heard the news that he had lost everything, this is how he responded: "Then Job arose and tore his robe and shaved his head and fell on the ground and *worshiped*. And he said, 'Naked I came from my mother's womb, and naked shall I return. The LORD gave, and the LORD has taken away; blessed be the name of the LORD'" (Job 1:20-21).

Likewise, when David's infant son died, he responded this way: "Then David arose from the earth and washed and anointed himself and changed his clothes. And he went into the house of the LORD and *worshiped*" (2 Samuel 12:20).

We do not just worship God when we have it all together, and the roses are blossoming. We also worship Him when everything is breaking, and the flowers have all withered. When we lose our camels, our houses, our children…our husbands.

Because what makes God worthy of praise has nothing to do with our circumstances. What makes God worthy of praise is simply who He is. It is His intrinsic character—His infinite wisdom, might, and power; His boundless grace, and mercy, and love. It is His justice and sovereignty, His goodness and holiness.

Those things never change. And neither does our worship.

Faithful friends that they were, the pastors who were available sat in my bedroom around Matt's body and prayed. Together, we worshipped the God who had given us Matt for so long and thanked Him for His goodness in Matt's life and in his death.

The funeral home people eventually arrived.

There was more sorrow as I removed his beloved GPS watch that had been so useful to him as he trekked across mountains in the jungle.

Then, they wheeled him out of our house in a body bag, another surreal moment.

As the day wound down and my dear friends returned to their own families, having lent their hands and strength to mine, I reflected on God's provision for me that day.

I had made it.

But not on my own.

God had given me the fortitude to watch my husband die, the strength to walk my children through losing their dad, and the grace to worship Him through it all.

Yes, it had been a terrible day.

I was still walking through a dark valley. And now I was walking without Matt by my side.

But I had a Good Shepherd.

And He had not left me today, though Matt had.

I still had Him, and with that, I still had everything.

This day, on July 18th, was *still* mercy and grace to myself and my children.

I did not deserve one day of love and laughter with Matt Dodd, and He had given me *thousands*.

I did not deserve one person to love and support my family throughout this whole ordeal, and He had given me *hundreds* in our church body and beyond.

But most of all, on July 18th of 2017, I was still forgiven, still loved, still freed from my sin.

I still had an imperishable, undefiled, and unfading inheritance to look forward to.

I would still, one day, get to see my Savior face-to-face.

And so it was I could still say at the end of that day, "Today is the day that the Lord has made. I will rejoice and be glad in it."

Part III

The Man Who Died Best

CHAPTER 23

Triumph

For a long time while I was writing this book, the working title was *The Man Who Died Well*.

I believe my husband was a remarkable man in some ways, able to combine a radical joy for life with a genuine steadfastness of faith, even in the midst of suffering.

But in most other ways, Matt was just a regular guy with struggles, shortcomings, and failures.

Yes, Matt Dodd did die better than I thought possible.

But to stop there would be to miss the point of this book entirely.

Letting the last pages of this narrative end on Matt would be like admiring an intricate portrait without asking whose fingers drew it.

Because Matt's life and death were never about him.

The truth that sings from Matt's lips in these pages, over and over, is that his hope was never in his own strength or resolve or health or family—it was all in the God who made him and saved him.

Matt Dodd was only able to be a man who died well because of the man who died best: Jesus Christ.

He was dead in his trespasses; Jesus had made him alive!

He was a slave to his sin; Jesus set him free!

He was a sheep hopelessly lost; Jesus came to seek and save the lost!

He made Matt Dodd and knew just where to find him when he was at his most lost. The day Matt looked to him to be saved, Jesus became his Shepherd, and—oh!—what a Good Shepherd He was.

He said, "I am the good shepherd. The good shepherd lays down his life for the sheep" (John 10:10-11).

He gave up His life that Matt might gain his. And He had been leading Matt ever since, through trial after trial, giving him the grace to endure, and making his faith a little more steadfast through each one. He never let Matt go, but faithfully upheld him until the time came to bring Matt home.

Matt's life, his death, and his joy were never about him but about the One who made him, saved him, and sustained him until the end.

In every trial, Matt looked back to the cross to remind himself what he had been saved *from*, and forward to heaven to remind himself of what he had been saved *to*. With Calvary in one hand, heaven in the other, and the grace of God beside him, he was able to endure through any circumstance.

He didn't become that way overnight, of course.

There was a grace-fueled faithfulness here.

A morning-by-morning effort not just to read the Bible, but to come to know the One who had written it. And as he persisted in this, he came to know Him a great deal.

He came to know Him as One who is good and does good (Ps. 119:68), One who is sovereign over all things (Is. 45:7-9), One who loved him (Rom. 8:35-39), gave His life to save him (Jn.3:16), and promised to work all things for his good (Rom. 8:28).

Jesus said in John 10:27-28, "My sheep hear my voice, and I know them, and they follow me. I give them eternal life, and they will never perish, and no one will snatch them out of my hand."

Matt knew Jesus' voice and followed Him, day after day, year after year. And in so doing, he was increasingly able to reflect His character to a watching world.

This is what he did on the campus of ASU, on the boardwalk of Santa Cruz, and on the streets of East Asia.

This is what he did at every supporting church he visited in the United States and every hut he slept in in Papua New Guinea.

This is what he did from the first day I met him until the last and what he did with each of our four kids.

And this is what he still did while paralyzed in a hospital bed and as he lay dying in our room.

Matt's life was not first and foremost, evidence of a faithful man—but of a faithful God!

He was only a sheep pointing others to his Good Shepherd; only a ray of sunshine, directing others to the Source of the light within him.

But there are lessons to be learned from this man's life.

The first of which is that, for the believer, perseverance is possible.

In this broken world, there are horrific, catastrophic, unthinkably tragic things that happen. And responding well, with faith and hope in God, seems impossible.

It's not.

Before Matt got sick, we saw faithful friends in our church walk through hard things with just that kind of faith and hope.

And since the writing of this book, I have watched still others walk through circumstances unfathomably difficult and still hold to that same message—"Yes! God is still good!"

Matt was an ordinary man who built his life on an extraordinary God, who did not fail him.

Perseverance in trials is not only possible for the believer; it is necessary! Because that is how we honor Christ!

Paul's aim was that "Christ will be honored in my body, whether by life or by death" (Phil. 1:20). And we ask, how do we that? How do we honor Christ by our life or death?

The answer is found in the next verse: "For to me to live is Christ, and *to die is gain*." Christ is honored when we make our life all about His glory, and when we look death in the eye and say, "*Gain!*"

Because it is!

Is the gospel enough? For the loss of a ministry? The loss of your health? The loss of your own life?

Yes!

Disaster doesn't change our sins being forgiven. Tragedy cannot alter God's love for us. Catastrophe can't touch our eternal inheritance in Christ.

Everything that is true in the gospel before that day of bad news still stands the day after.

Perseverance is possible.

The second lesson to be learned from Matt's life is that tomorrow is not guaranteed.

Matt was a 36-year-old, healthy, strong, man hiking all over what is quite possibly the most difficult terrain on the planet.

He ran. He hiked. He did yoga.

He brushed his teeth for two minutes every day.

And by the time he was diagnosed, he only had six months left to live.

We will all live and work and then, one day, perhaps unexpectedly, we, too, will draw our last breath.

If you do not know this kind of hope, if you don't understand joy in these circumstances, if you do not have this kind of confidence in what lies beyond the grave, if you have not yet had come to Jesus Christ to have your sins forgiven—

Dear reader, can I plead with you to consider these things?

Matt Dodd was only able to have this kind of hope and joy because it was rooted in Jesus Christ. In His character; in His promises.

There is no hope outside of this. Jesus said, "I am *the* way, *the* truth, and *the* life. No one comes to the Father except through me" (John 14:6).

Would you consider that this offer of salvation, this offer of redemption, this offer of forgiveness and mercy and hope and grace and *joy* goes out to you as well?

Would you consider making the God of Matt Dodd your own?

*　　　　*　　　　*　　　　*

Hallmark movies always end the same way.

Whatever conflict that may have existed between the two main characters suddenly gets resolved in the last two minutes of the movie, leaving you to wonder, "Did it last?"

It's been over six years since Matt died, as of the writing of this book, and you might be wondering, "Sure, God was faithful during a very difficult season…but did it last?"

Dear reader, the answer is yes.

God has not left me or forsaken me for one moment over the years.

He has been *my* Good Shepherd, leading me, teaching me, pulling me back when I wander too far.

Trials are hard, and death is painful, but it was an absolute privilege to go through what I have gone through.

Because I have gotten to see God be who He says He is and do what He promises to do in a way I never would have gotten to see otherwise.

I have gotten to watch Him keep every promise He made to my husband and faithfully finish the work He had begun in him so many years ago.

And I have seen Him in the years since care for me and meet me in every moment of weakness, just the same as He did the day Matt died.

God has done me no wrong; He has done my children no wrong. In fact, He has only done us good.

Psalm 84:11 says, "For the LORD God is a sun and shield; the LORD bestows favor and honor. **No good thing** does he withhold from those who walk uprightly."

God does not withhold anything good from those He loves.

During his funeral sermon, George Mueller said this of his wife's illness:

> "When I heard what the doctor's judgment was, viz., that the malady was rheumatic fever, I naturally expected the worst as to the issue; but though my heart was nigh to be broken, on account of the depth of my affection, I said to myself, *"The Lord is good; and doeth good,"* all will be according to His own blessed character.
>
> "Nothing but that, which is good, like Himself, can proceed from Him. If He pleases to take my dearest wife, it will be good, like Himself. What I have to do, as His child, is to be satisfied with what my Father does, that I may glorify Him. After this my soul not only

aimed at, but this, my soul, by God's grace, attained to. I was satisfied with God."

God has been pleased to rescue me from a life of hopeless despair. He is my Father who does only good towards His children.

He is also infinitely wise—do I, a mere piece of clay, know better than the Maker and Sustainer of the universe? Surely not.

"He who did not spare his own Son but gave him up for us all, how will he not also with him graciously give us all things?" (Romans 8:32).

He spared not His own Son!

Were there something better for myself or my children, He would surely give it!

It was not because of a lack of power on God's part that Matt died. Surely, the God who spoke light into darkness and raised Lazarus with a word could have healed Matt.

No, Matt died because God had one plan and one purpose to accomplish in his life, and on July 18th, 2017, that purpose was perfectly accomplished.

This isn't to say it is not still hard sometimes.

And in those hard moments, there is a temptation to take my eyes off of Jesus and fix them on my circumstances. In those moments, I open my Bible and remind myself that I need to pry my grieving eyes off my circumstances and fix them on the One who was put to grief for me.

What was true before Matt died is still true today. That Rock has not moved from under me; that rope still holds me fast.

What I lost in my husband was great.

But what I have still is greater.

Because what I said to those precious faces in that closet is true: I still have Jesus, and, in Him, I still have everything.

There are those who might hear of these circumstances for a thirty-six-year-old father of four in the midst of an overseas mission and say "tragedy".

And for one whose hope and stock are in this world, that would be irrefutably true.

But Matt was not one of those.

His hope and his stock were not in this world, but somewhere else entirely.

Matt sang his last verse on this earth and woke up to sing it anew for eternity—in the presence of the very One about whom he sang! He finally got to receive that imperishable, undefiled, and unfading inheritance!

And as he would tell you, that is simply not tragedy.

It is triumph.

Made in the USA
Las Vegas, NV
29 April 2024

89287642R00156